DO NOT REMOVE
CARDS FROM POCKET

Football Coach Quotes

Football Coach Quotes

*The Wit, Wisdom and Winning Words
of Leaders on the Gridiron*

Compiled by
Larry Adler

McFarland & Company, Inc., Publishers
Jefferson, North Carolina, and London

British Library Cataloguing-in-Publication data are available

Library of Congress Cataloguing-in-Publication Data

Football coach quotes : the wit, wisdom and winning words of leaders
  on the gridiron / compiled by Larry Adler.
     p.   cm.
   Includes bibliographical references (p. 195) and index.
   ISBN 0-89950-542-2 (lib. bdg. : 50# alk. paper) ⊚
   1. Football—United States—Quotations, maxims, etc.   2. Football—
United States—Coaches—Quotations.   I. Adler, Larry, 1939- .
GV959.F56   1992
796.332'0973—dc20   91-52630
                                                                           CIP

©1992 Larry Adler. All rights reserved

Manufactured in the United States of America

McFarland & Company, Inc., Publishers
  Box 611, Jefferson, North Carolina 28640

*To my uncles
Abe, Izzy, Norman and Saul*

Table of Contents

Preface

When I first got the idea for this book, it was only going to contain words quoted from Vince Lombardi. Then I started doing my research, and, just out of curiosity, began to check out what Knute Rockne, Bear Bryant and other famous coaches had written or said. I liked what I found and discovered that compiling quotes from football coaches was like dipping into hot buttered popcorn. Once you start, you just can't stop.

So I changed direction. Now my book was going to contain quotes from not just Lombardi, but any famous coach. But the quotes were virtually all going to be motivational, inspirational, the kind an executive might put on a plaque on a wall in his office and repeat to himself whenever he needed a shot of mental adrenalin.

I continued with my research. I really started to dig. I came across sayings by an Ed. D. (LaVell Edwards), an artist (Robert Zuppke), a Casey Stengel sound-alike (Joe Kuharich), a Phi Beta Kappa (Marv Levy), a dentist (Jock Sutherland), a musician who wrote a team fight song (Jimmy Conzelman), a foreman in a coal yard (Steve Owen), a Shakespearian actor (John Heisman), people with law degrees, doctors, successful businessmen, officers in the military—even an ex–pro wrestler (Herman Hickman). I came across quotes by compassionate caring leaders as well as harsh slave drivers. I came across the thoughts of people who might qualify as modern day philosophers. And, thank goodness, I came across quotes that put a smile on my face—quips and one-liners that time and again demonstrated that a coach can maintain his sense of humor despite the tremendous and continual pressure to win, win, win.

So I changed direction again. Now my book was not only going to contain quotes about success, persistence and achievement, it was also going to contain quotes about—well, anything. Friendship. Religion. Growing older. If the quote looked good on paper, if it sounded OK when I said it out loud, I decided to include it in this book.

I also decided my book was now going to contain material from the widest possible range of coaches—the famous, the not-so-famous, leaders with outstanding won-loss records, leaders with poor won-loss records,

Catholics, Jews, old-timers, present-dayers, whites, blacks, Ivy Leaguers, Big Ten coaches, coaches who'd spent time in the Canadian Football League, and even one assistant coach. The latter is unique, the only member of the 7,000-strong American Football Coaches Association who is a woman.

If I hadn't expanded my inclusion criteria, if I hadn't decided to include interesting quotes no matter who they came from, I would have left out a lot of good sayings and a lot of good people. Herman Hickman, to pick a prime example: He only coached for four years. He wound up with a losing record. But what an intellect! What an interesting background (a pro wrestler!). And what a wit. How could I have left him out?

I compiled quotes from the standard resources—newspapers, magazines and books—in the standard way any researcher would go about tackling any research project—visiting the library, parking myself on a seat and going through whatever material I could get my hands on.

I included a few quotes from rousing half-time locker room pep talks that rallied athletes and sent them charging back on the field with renewed fire and determination. (Read those quotes and maybe, just maybe, you'll get a sense of the incredible power those words had on their listeners.)

I included some quotes that are rather long instead of short and pithy. If it took 100 or even 200 words for the coach to make his point or express an interesting view, so be it. I didn't try to avoid quotes about controversial subjects that are part of the game—drugs and illegal college recruiting, for instance. But I kept them to a minimum.

If this book contains any words that in and of themselves are controversial, I'd say they were the two most famous quotes in this book: "Winning isn't everything, it's the only thing" from Vince Lombardi and Rockne's "Win one for the Gipper" speech.

How could they be controversial? Let's take "Winning isn't everything" first. According to some sources, Lombardi wasn't the first to coin that phrase; it was Red Sanders, who said it while a coach at UCLA in the early 1950s. According to other sources, Lombardi claimed he never made the statement. What he actually said, according to the great coach himself, was "Winning isn't everything, but wanting to win is." However another source quoted Lombardi as saying he'd wished he'd never made the oft-quoted remark. That's an admission that he said it. I decided to attribute the famous quote to Lombardi. Why? Because it's associated with him and nobody else.

Next, Rockne's "Win one for the Gipper" speech, supposedly delivered during halftime of the 1928 Army–Notre Dame game, when the contest was a scoreless tie. (Notre Dame went on to win, 12–6.) The controversy here is that a few sources doubt the speech was made (I think it was), and even if it was delivered, various sources cannot agree on Rockne's exact words. To prove the point, my "Win one for the Gipper" quote is different from the one included in Andrew J. Maikovich's 1984 *Sports Quotations*, which is also available from McFarland.

In some cases, reading all the quotable words from a particular coach can be likened to reading a minibiography. When combined, they can tell you something about the individual's life and give you an insight into his thoughts and personality. That information may make you want to find out more about a person. To help you do so, I've included a reading list at the back of the book.

The book also contains a thorough index, a vital necessity for those using the book as a research tool.

My plan was to preface each coach's quotes with: the teams he was associated with, the years he was associated with each team, and his overall won-loss record, or, if he was still coaching, his record up to the end of the 1989 season. In some cases, this information proved to be elusive. Therefore in some cases, the preface to a coach's quotes contains some, but not all, of the above-mentioned information.

Whether you're a football fan, a speechwriter looking for a quote to illustrate a point, an individual looking for a mantra for self-motivation, or just a browser, I hope you enjoy and gain some benefit from all that follows.

Larry Adler
Fall 1991

The Winning Words (by Coach)

Fred Akers

Coach: University of Wyoming 1975–1976, University of Texas 1977–1986, Purdue 1987– . Record: 106-66-3.

1 Get out the wide angle lens, boys, I'm getting ready to smile.

2 Lou Holtz can talk faster than I can listen.

3 Sometimes progress comes very slowly, but it sure makes you appreciate it when it gets here.

4 I'm in favor of having year-round random testing for steroids. Once-a-year testing at bowl games is not enough.

5 When I was in school they gave us, as part of our scholarship, a small amount of money, $15 a month for incidental expenses. That wouldn't buy soap for laundry now.

6 Football doesn't take me away from my family life. We've always watched films together.

7 Proposition 48 has given us a better gauge of who should and shouldn't be allowed into college.

William A. "Bill" Alexander

Coach: Georgia Tech 1920–1944. Record: 134-95-15.

8 Every step he takes is to our advantage — *said when Roy Riegels of the University of California ran the wrong way during 1929 Rose Bowl.*

9   They will beat us nine times out of ten, but in losing we will learn a lot of football. We will gain a lot of prestige nationally. And when we win, it will be a mighty sweet victory—*said of playing Notre Dame.*

10   The better team will win in the mud but not by as wide a margin as on a dry field. We are the better team.

George H. Allen

Coach: Morningside College 1948–1950, Whittier College 1951–1956, Los Angeles Rams 1966–1970, Washington Redskins 1971–1977, Chicago Blitz (USFL) 1983, Arizona Outlaws (USFL) 1984. Record: 191-104-12.

11   Every time you win, you're reborn. Any time you lose, you die a little.

12   We were not put on this earth to enjoy ourselves.

13   The future is now.

14   We know what we have to do. They know what we can do.

15   The man who can accept defeat and take his salary without feeling guilty is a thief.

16   Leisure time is that five or six hours when you sleep at night.

17   It has been said that we're born for pain, that if we don't come into the world crying, the doctor spanks us until we start.

18   Just prior to the kickoff, the players will pair up on the sidelines and go through the following routine. They will pound each other three or four times with their fists on their shoulder pads, possibly a smack once on the side of the helmet. These are usually not love pats but hard blows to loosen each other up and knock out some of the butterflys.

19   Another game has gone into the books, but the cycle starts all over again. Football is back to work.

20   Vodka and Valium. The breakfast of champions—*referring to the reason why he cut John Matuszak.*

21   The most dangerous thing you can do is get your eleven fastest men and put them on the kickoff cover team and let them all go for the ball. Kickoffs should be covered in waves.

22   Today's brand of winning football requires total commitment. I do not believe you can win by working only from 9 to 5.

23   When I was coaching at Washington, the Redskins agreed, at my request, to furnish me with a car and driver. Some people suggested I was looking for more than an easy way to get around: they thought the car was for taking me on ego trips. But I have found that one of the keys to success in coaching was full utilization of time. There is always more time available to do a job than appears, if you manage your time properly. I wanted a driver so I could get some work done while on the road.

24   Tell me how a person uses his time and I'll tell you whether I want to hire him.

25   If you love your work, it's really no longer work.

26   I always avoid loud exits. Slamming the door behind you could close doors ahead of you.

27   It doesn't do any good to play in the Super Bowl if you don't win.

28   I can't get out of here fast enough—*said after '73 Super Bowl loss to Miami, 14–7.*

29   I learned long ago that I loved coaching more than anything but my family.

30   In order to do all the things that I want to do with my work, I have to have a wife like mine who will put up with my being away from home so much.

31   Work is simply a synonym for effort. A 100 percent effort is not enough. The world belongs to those who aim for 110 percent.

32   He said he was sorry—*referring to Duane Thomas, who grabbed and threatened an assistant coach who wanted him to stay after practice to see a game film.*

33   One thing I've learned is that you must fight all your life for everything.

34   You cannot rest on yesterday's accomplishments.

35   No detail is too small if part of an important undertaking. Knowing your work in detail is knowing what you're doing.

36   Without goals, where does one head?

37   An effective way to motivate a football team is the use of slogans. We have found them to be of significant value in emphasizing various points in our training and organization.

38   Football is a rough, tough, bruising game and if a boy doesn't like body contact and being knocked down, he shouldn't get into it.

39   To be a successful football player, a lineman must have a strong desire for bodily contact, to want to knock somebody down. We like the overly aggressive type who can also take it.

40   Defensive linemen must be aggressive, alert and mean.

41   The great passers have the courage to hold onto the football until the last split second before throwing it. They are able to stand back in the pocket and take some occasional punishment.

42   Those damn Cowboys. I can't stand them in those pretty, clean, shiny uniforms. When we get done with them, they won't be pretty, clean or shiny.

43   They're on approval. If they don't fit, they go back—*referring to the method the too-busy-to-shop coach uses to buy his clothes—they're sent to him after being selected by his wife.*

44   I want to look in my locker room and see bald, old men; guys who have been through it—winners.

45   Yelling and screaming is not my style. I do not believe in tearing down. I believe in building up.

46   While a coach can be tough, he should also be human.

47   There are not many people who enjoy being criticized in front of 50 or 60 people. It is much better to talk to them alone.

48   The toughest moments of coaching are in the individual conferences with players going over their problems—not football problems.

49   The biggest mistake linebackers make is committing too soon. Middle linebackers must learn to bounce in place until they're sure of the route to take to the ball carrier. Outside linebackers have an axiom, "When in doubt, shuffle out!"

50   Once in awhile center back a wet ball without the kicker's knowledge—*referring to a way to keep kickers on their toes during practice.*

51   I was extremely explicit with the contractor. I told him "I don't want a fourth place house. I don't want a third place house. I don't want a second place house. I want a championship house." You're looking at a championship house.

52   A football coach has to be a salesman. He must sell not only himself but the sport, as well.

53   It isn't bad enough to just go out and beat someone. You've got to want to annihilate them. You've got to bury them, you've got to bust them up.

54   Organization is the foundation of all successful football coaching.

55   Winning is the science of being totally prepared.

56   They don't make reusable days.

57   Reason, not emotion, should rule your life.

58   If you're not a puppet, you're in trouble—*referring to a coach's relationship with club owners and off-field executives.*

59   Exercise is excellent therapy for depression.

60   A workout is a personal triumph over laziness and procrastination.

61   Without some kind of release, a tense person is soon apt to become a past-tense person.

62   A team fails on the field. We may not know for sure whose fault it is, but we know who's going to get fired—the coach.

63   Developing the art of faking should be the prime concern of every quarterback. With little feints in his hands, arms and body, he can make defenders move in the wrong direction.

64   Fakers are not good fakers unless they can attract defenders.

65   Offense requires skill; defense requires frenzy.

66   I think of what has to be done, not of whether it can be done.

67   We win and lose as a team.

68   I believe that everything in life has a purpose. And our lives themselves have a purpose. Organizing the details of our lives brings that purpose into sharper focus. The sharper it is, the less likely we will lose sight of it after a severe setback.

69   Organization is a habit.

70   A person without problems is dead.

71   A problem is only a problem when you cannot solve it. The winning coach is a successful problem solver.

72   Coaching football is the greatest profession in the world and I would not trade it for anything.

Dr. Edward N. Anderson

Coach: Loras College 1922, De Paul University 1925–1931, Holy Cross 1933–1938 and 1950–1964, University of Iowa 1939–1942 and 1946–1949. Record: 201-128-15.

73   We had it cinched with that first safety but we wanted to run up the score—*said after his team won a game, 4–0, with two safeties.*

Madison A. "Matty" Bell

Coach: Haskell Institute 1920–1921, Carroll (Wisconsin) 1922, Texas Christian 1923–1928, Texas A&M 1929–1933, SMU 1935–1941 and 1945–1949. Record: 154-87-17.

74   Alumni have strange reasoning. They fire a coach instead of giving him sufficient material to produce a team that can win, and when they get hot enough to wield the axe, they usually are aroused enough at the same time to provide material for the new one, who then turns out a good workmanlike job and is called a wizard.

75   Marvelous coaching jobs are usually marvelous amounts of work, thought, application and getting the maximum out of the material at hand. Any expert diamond cutter, laboriously, painstakingly and with delicate craftsmanship, can trim the uneven stone which nature gave him, and polish the facets to gleaming brilliance, but I never heard of anyone doing it with a hunk of coal.

76   I thought someone was being mobbed. Someone was. It was us! Lining up on the tracks, delaying the train, blocking traffic for one-half a mile, jammed like a sea of sardines, 25,000 Dallas people were there to give a conqueror's welcome to warriors being brought home on our shields. That, I thought, was the kind of alumni that counted—*said after his team lost the 1935 Rose Bowl.*

77   What I should have done was to have banned banquets, abolished autographs and taken the team into the desert until the day of the game—*said after losing Rose Bowl.*

Raymond E. "Ray" Berry

Coach: New England Patriots 1984–1989. Record: 54-38.

78   It was a crucial Baltimore–Green Bay Packer game. The Western Division title was riding on the outcome. It was third and six, the Colts had the ball inside the Packer 30-yard line, threatening and needing one touchdown to go ahead late in the fourth quarter. Willie Davis, the great Packer defensive end, was fighting to get to Unitas in an effort to force an incompletion. A Colt receiver broke open over the middle with clear sailing to the goal line. Davis was closing in on Unitas with great effort. Unitas released the ball, but just as he did Willie Davis managed to barely get a piece of the ball. It wasn't very much, but it took some of the trajectory off the throw. The receiver had to slow down slightly and reach down for a low pass. This delay turned a potential touchdown into a 20-yard gain and a first down. On the next play, the Colts fumbled, the Packers recovered and then ran out the clock. If Willie Davis had been just a few inches later, Baltimore would have won. It's a game of inches.

79   There is a certain amount of pain and suffering involved in getting into good shape.

80   What I learned the hard way is that there are some physical laws that you don't break—they break you.

81   Here is a statement that I read once and believe to be true: "Confidence is the end product of a mastered skill."

82   I don't rightly know, but she runs the projector—*reply when asked if his fiancée could cook.*

83   It's almost like a marriage. You have to make allowances and understand each other. You get to know each other so well that you know instinctively what to expect in any situation—*said about the relationship between a passer and receiver.*

84   A receiver catching a pass over the middle is separated from the football more frequently than a catch near the sideline.

85   A receiver who goes at full speed only when he is the intended receiver is a liability to the offensive unit.

86   In your preparations and practices, your players never know which detail they are working on will be the one that wins a game for you. Every practice, every meeting is important.

87   A longtime axiom in football has been, "Have a plan for everything and practice it."

88   .The wide receiver position is unique. No other position has caused defenses to adjust so many ways to contain it.

89   Every defensive alignment will give up something in order to be in a position to stop something else.

90   Catching the long ball is the most advanced part of the receiver's art.

91   Mental fatigue can be just as damaging to the athlete as physical fatigue.

92   Attitudes can be altered.

Hugo F. Bezdek

Coach: University of Oregon 1906 and 1913–1917, University of Arkansas 1908–1912, Penn State 1918–1929, Los Angeles Rams 1937–1938, National Agricultural College 1949. Record: 132-75-16.

93   The best team lost. A football team with the best coaching in the world could not win against the luck the Trojans had — *said after losing Rose Bowl, 14–3, to University of Southern California, in 1923.*

94   Perhaps I'd do better if you cussed me out — *said during his playing days to his coach, Amos Alonzo Stagg, who never swore.*

Dana X. Bible

Coach: Mississippi College 1913–1915, Louisiana State 1916, Texas A&M 1917 and 1919–1928, University of Nebraska 1929–1936, University of Texas 1937–1946. Record: 198-72-23.

95   I used to tell the fellows if they would pay the premiums they would get the dividends.

Jack Bicknell

Coach: University of Maine 1976–1980, Boston College 1981– . Record: 73-83-2.

96   What's the worst thing that could happen to me? I could get fired.

I might get hit with a tomato from the stands. So what?—*said when he left Maine for BC.*

97   I believe in a quarterback-oriented offense. You do what your quarterback can do.

98   If we lose, the sun's still going to come up.

99   This is the way football used to be played out in the ice and cold. Now they have all these domes and I'm not sure that's football. You have to be able to adjust to any kind of weather or condition.

Bernard W. "Bernie" Bierman

Coach: University of Montana 1919–1921, Mississippi State 1925–1926, Tulane 1927–1931, University of Minnesota 1932–1941 and 1945–1950. Record: 163-57-11.

100   I don't think I'd be able to make a sentimental dressing room talk. I'm afraid I would end up laughing at myself.

101   Two touchdowns will win it—*his entire halftime pep talk to a Minnesota team losing, 7–0—the team went back, held Pittsburgh scoreless and beat them with the two touchdowns Bierman asked for.*

102   The Marine Corps taught me discipline, and organization, and to love life.

103   Despite the storybooks, there is no such thing anymore as the flash who drives through for the winning touchdown in the first game he enters. Every lad you see on successive Saturdays during the season is the product of weeks and months of rigid, painstaking training.

104   Walk out there, and expend your energy after you get out there— *said to Tulane team rushing onto field.*

105   When I have to beg a kid of 16 or 17 to go out for football, then I'll quit.

106   But I know how fickle a fan can be.

107   A boy who places personal glory and success above the best interests of the team is a liability rather than an asset.

108   A large, fairly well-developed squad is more desirable than a team composed of a few stars and a group of mediocre, undeveloped talent.

109   We believe that fundamentals such as blocking, charging, tackling and ball carrying, to mention only a few, are more important than plays themselves.

110   We favor a calm, determined team rather than one keyed up to a hysterical pitch for a game.

111   I'm lucky somebody didn't shoot me this first week—*said after harsh practice.*

Earl H. "Red" Blaik

Coach: Dartmouth 1934–1940, West Point 1941–1958. Record: 166-48-14.

112   There is no substitute for work. It is the price of success.

113   I don't want anyone limping through a workout. If you have to limp, don't work out. But if you work out, don't limp.

114   The essence of the game, the only "fun" of the game, is the soul-satisfying awareness that comes not only with victory but also with the realization that victory more than justifies all the communal work and sacrifice that went into it.

115   Young men respect authority and a football team cannot be coached by committee action.

116   He is volatile, enthusiastic and given to degrees of emotion not likely to be found in a coach—*said of Vince Lombardi.*

117   A coach who comes in at the bottom of a curve has a pronounced advantage over one who succeeds to a going or even half-going operation. In 1941, there was no place to go at West Point but up.

118   It was here "the brave old Army team" stood fast like the Federals of General George Thomas at Chickamauga—*said of a successful Army goal line stand.*

119   We were fighting for our lives—*said of a hard game.*

120   Blanchard and Davis were the best 1-2 punch, in my belief, that college football ever saw—*referring to Doc Blanchard and Glenn Davis, who played for him in the mid–1940s.*

121   Who was the best of the two? I never separated them—*said of Blanchard and Davis.*

122   He was not so much a dodger and a sidestepper as a blazing runner who had a fourth and even a fifth gear in reserve, could change direction at top speed and fly away from tacklers as if jet-propelled—*said of Glenn Davis.*

123   I was just as concerned about that injured man as you were. But to be consoling an injured man is bad for you and bad for him. It breeds a softness that is inimical to success.

124   You have to pay the price.

125   I always drove my assistants as hard as I drove myself. Our families saw little of us, part of the price of our mission and the steepest part of all.

126   Very simple—the position of the quarterback's feet told Carpenter what the play would be—*referring to Bill Carpenter, the "lonely end," who didn't join the rest of the team in the huddle, lined up far away from everyone else and needed to know Army's plans.*

127   You don't develop good teeth by eating mush.

128   There never was a champion who to himself was a good loser. There's a vast difference between a good sport and a good loser.

129   Good fellows are a dime a dozen but an aggressive leader is priceless.

130   Inches make a champion and a champion makes his own luck.

131   It's a rarity when an individual can take successive years of the pressure of this sort of thing.

132   All they had to do was refuse to answer or to plead innocence. To them this would have been dishonorable—*referring to cadets who admitted knowing about cheating by other cadets, (they didn't do it themselves), who were also dismissed during cheating scandal at West Point—1951.*

133   I could not, try as I would, coach with my normal enthusiasm, drive and patience—*said after scandal.*

134   I have to give you a choice in this. If you say "no," you can be an All-American end for a second year and I'll understand. But we have no leader and no quarterback and I want you to be both—*said to Don Holleder, an All-American in his junior year, after West Point cheating scandal almost wiped out Army football team. Holleder said "yes" to Blaik's request.*

135   Games are not won on the rubbing table.

136   They had lived under the coaching lash, with dirt, blood and constant defeat—*said of Army team in '53, two years after team was decimated by cheating scandal.*

137   I had to convince our team that they not only could be, but should be, winners. I myself was far from convinced for a long, long time that what I was trying to sell them was actually the truth. But I knew I must still try to sell them. And the strange thing is, I not only convinced them, but by the end of the season they convinced me—*said of '53 team.*

138   We couldn't stop their passing and they couldn't stop our running—*said of game in which Army beat Colgate, 55–46.*

139   Football is a marvelous game because of its limitless permutations and combinations of men in action.

140   This game is different from the rest. And if you lose you have the whole winter to think about it—*said of annual Army-Navy football games.*

141   When you get to my age, you don't think of health—*said in 1985 when he was nearly 90.*

142   We've made mistakes in the game. Biggest has been the isolation of the players, having them live together and eat together as though they were set apart from the rest of the students.

143   The game is complex; players must be intelligent.

144   There's no end to ideas. I sleep with a pad alongside my bed.

145   I don't think it is my prerogative or my affair—*referring to choosing his successor.*

146   Our major problem at Dartmouth was to replace the spirit of good fellowship, which is antithetical to successful football, with the Spartanism that is indispensable. The successful coach is one who can sell the Spartan approach, the one who is able to get a willing acceptance from his men that victory or success demands a special price.

147   We'll be as successful as you men will let us. If there is anybody in this room who is not ready to do some strong sacrificing, I hope we've seen him for the last time.

Bobby Bowden

Coach: Stanford 1959–1962, University of West Virginia 1970–1975, Florida State University 1976– . Record: 195-72-3.

148   Are we supposed to brag? Not brag? Play humble? — *said before the start of the '88 season, after being proclaimed the best team in the country by the Associated Press and various football magazines.*

149   We celebrated too early — *said after losing first game of '88 season.*

150   I've always said, kind of jokingly, and I don't know if I mean it or not, "Boy, I'd like to be so good we'd get investigated and not be guilty." Because when you're investigated, that's a good sign. You must be pretty good.

151   I'd just hate for my players and people associated with my program to hear people say, "Y'all won, but y'all cheated."

152   If it was, Army and Navy would be playing for the national championship every year — *reply when asked if discipline was the key to winning.*

153   He doesn't know the meaning of the word "fear." In fact, I just saw his grades and he doesn't know the meaning of a lot of words.

154   We'll play at 2:00 A.M. if they wanted us to — *referring to television executives.*

Paul E. Brown

Coach: Ohio State 1941–1943, Cleveland Browns 1946–1962, Cincinnati Bengals 1968–1975. Record: 268-160-10.

155   Winning makes believers of us all.

156   We have just one objective — to win.

157   Always remember, when you meet an obnoxious football player, the meanest thing you can do to him is beat him. They can play dirty, call you names, violate the rules. Just beat 'em. They understand that more than anything.

158   I was strong-willed and single-minded and possessed a fierce sense of independence. I believed strongly in the things that were necessary for us to win, and I refused to tolerate any exceptions to those beliefs.

159   In this is the true artistry in my profession: the ability to do the right thing at the right time at the right place for the greatest possible number of times under the stress of a game.

160   I run everything here. If something goes wrong, don't bother to complain to your teammates or the assistant coaches or the president of the club. They can't help you. I'm the only one.

161   Complete control. There is no other way for a team to operate and be a winner.

162   If I had hired me at that time, I'd have done it and then gotten far away.

163   They talk about Super Bowl records today. The NFL championship game was our Super Bowl and we played in it seven times the first eight years we were in the league—*said of his days with the Cleveland Browns.*

164   When you have the big gun, you pull the trigger—*reply when asked why running back Jim Brown carried the ball so much in a game.*

165   You finish last ten years in a row. Then you get Vince Lombardi to put all those first draft choices together—*reply when asked how to develop a championship team.*

166   You are a member of the Cleveland Browns. You are the New York Yankees of football. You will conduct yourself in a proper manner. I expect you to watch your language, your dress, your deportment.

167   I expect civilized table manners and table talk. There have been people who have failed to make this team simply because they were obnoxious to eat with.

168   Save yourself for the game—*referring to his "Tuesday Rule"—no sex after Tuesday when a game was on Sunday.*

169   That young man did not understand how I feel about interceptions—*referring to why he traded a new quarterback.*

170   As a coach I never believed in working into the wee hours of the night. I personally functioned and thought more clearly when I was well rested, and I think a coaching staff does, too. I've heard some professional coaches brag about working 18 to 20 hours a day, sleeping on cots in their office and I've always wondered just how much they really accomplish during all those hours.

171   Coaches spend a lot more time preparing for an opponent than players generally do. Calling the plays was our way of controlling what we did on the day of the game. The artistic aspect of coaching is to manipulate a team under stress of combat rather than entrusting the responsibility to a player and risk the consequences. I preferred to do it myself.

172   Our coaches became the first in professional football ever to work year-round. There was no dignity, I felt, in having a man coach our offensive line for six months and then sell automobiles for six months.

173   Everything had to do with people—from properly assessing a man's character, intelligence and talent to getting him to perform to the best of his ability in a way that benefited the team.

174   We always preferred "raising our own"—drafting players we were sure of and who believed in our system.

175   There is nothing wrong with losing unless you learn to like it.

176   Try to lie and you lose the team.

177   Tomorrow it may be hot and we'll practice. Later there will be snow and we'll practice. It may be raining buckets and we'll practice. Soon you'll accept this as part of the routine and enjoy it.

178   If it's worth something, it's worth everything.

179   I enjoy winning and very much dislike losing—but I did not allow either of them to obsess me. I was a silent loser, believing that if you won, you said little, and if you lost, you said even less.

180   A victory at any price had no value for me, nor did I put down our team if it played well, yet lost.

181   We played a lot of teams that were beaten in their own minds even before the kickoff.

182   What are you doing, Quinlan—trying to ruin my organization? —*said to Bill Quinlan, caught smoking.*

183   We can lick any team that gets off a bus smoking cigars.

184   Keep your wives out of our football. Don't have your wife talk football with other wives. It breeds trouble. For example, I don't want one wife of a receiver complaining to the wife of the quarterback that her husband is being overlooked on pass plays.

185   People are going to be calling you names. They're going to be nasty, but you're going to have to stick it out—*said to Marion Motley and Bill Willis, black players who joined Cleveland in 1946.*

186   If he can't run, he can hop around—*reply to a trainer who suggested that an injured player should rest.*

187   The greatest back I ever had was Marion Motley. You know why? The only statistic he ever knew was whether we won or lost.

188   A pro football coach is a teacher, no matter what.

189   When we told our players "why," they were more willing to accept everything we asked them to do and to get into the spirit of the game. Good football requires that acquiescence.

190   I never left anything to their imagination: I laid out exactly what I expected from them, how I expected them to act on and off the field and what we expected to accomplish each day of the season.

191   If you sneak out after bed checks you'll be fined five hundred dollars and you'll read about it in the paper and I'll be the first to tell your wife—*said at training camp.*

192   There are too many good players from small schools to ignore their potential.

193   There is nothing incompatible in being a good person and being a hard-nosed football player.

194   I'm sure there were times when our players wondered if their old coach really knew how hard they tried or if he appreciated all their efforts.

195   There were no great mysteries attached to our success. We were meticulous in all our preparations, and we even practiced how to practice.

196   When you're lean and hungry, you fight the good fight.

197   We can't afford to get ripe. When you become ripe, the next step is to become rotten, and when you become rotten, you fall.

198   We knew their tackles were taught to line up opposite our tackles, and we reasoned that if we moved ours wider with each play, theirs would follow, and their middle guard would be isolated. With wider spacing along the defensive line, we could then run our trap plays with devastating effect.

199   No one could move him because of his bulk, so we developed a scheme of "influence blocking" in which we blocked him toward the area where we wanted to run the play, knowing that he'd react against the pressure and take himself out of the play—*referring to 325-pound Len Bingaman, middle guard for Lions.*

200   A perfectly executed pass play cannot fail. It cannot be adequately defended against, but you only get perfect execution part of the time.

201   Football is war, you know. And wars are won by the army that's fit and ready.

202   No one can be like anybody else.

203   I know I've gotten rid of some talented people. Even during my first season of coaching at Ohio State I got rid of a good player or two, simply because they wouldn't stick to the rules. One fellow went out night-clubbing the night before a game, and we just don't tolerate that sort of thing. So, for the future of our football and what-not, he was dismissed. And we went right along. So if that makes me a cold, hard person, I guess that's what I am. But you have to think of what is good for the team. You have to think of the future.

204   You run on your own gas; it comes from within you.

205   They have nothing to do at night but talk about you—*referring to his assistant coaches.*

206   It was the end of an era that could never again be duplicated because, though we tried, we never found another Otto Graham—*said after Graham retired in '55 as Browns quarterback.*

207   We always cut players as soon as we were sure they couldn't make the team.

208   We can't keep everybody.

209   I just could not bring myself to tell these men, whom I had known since they were boys, that their careers were over.

210   I'm philosophical about it—*said after 59–15 loss to Detroit.*

211   The ball was just going to bounce that way and it did—*said after same game.*

212   I don't want you to play for your check. I want you to play for the sheer desire of licking somebody.

213   You can't ask a guy to be something special if you don't treat him that way.

214   When I had my early meetings with a new player, I wanted his wife present so she'd know the role I expected of them both.

215   I don't believe in picking up a lot of old people.

216   I felt like a man starting a new family at age 59—*referring to when he began a new job coaching the Bengals.*

217   Don't ever leave it—*advice to Weeb Ewbank about coaching. Brown got paid for five years after leaving Cleveland Browns.*

218   I like chocolate cake but not every day for breakfast—*referring to all the time he had for recreation after leaving the Browns.*

219   You can get tired of a vacation.

220   That got things into focus in a hurry—*said when he was in Hong Kong and discovered no one knew about him or American football.*

221   Traveling the world gave me a perspective of myself.

222   Don't tell me you'll miss seeing me on the sidelines because I know you just like to see me suffer.

223   Getting into football is a state of heart and mind as well as physical.

224   It's a new season. We take nothing for granted.

225   I always told our players that any harsh words spoken during the heat of the game should be forgotten once the game ended because they usually rose more out of emotion than reason.

226   I made sure the player knew that he had made a mistake; I also made sure he knew I wasn't mad at him, and then we went on as if it hadn't happened.

227   I have always believed that young men want to work in an atmosphere of reasoned discipline and order and respond better under those conditions.

228   You make all sorts of plans, but sooner or later in any close game the unexpected always happens. You fool somebody or they fool you, and that's the ball game. Football would be awful dull if things turned out any other way.

229   The public is interested in only one thing—whether you win or lose.

230   It's a long, hard war.

J. Franklin "Frank" Broyles

Coach: University of Missouri 1957, University of Arkansas 1958–1976. Record: 149-62-6.

231   A 35-point lead just isn't safe anymore—*said after Arkansas, winning 35–0 at the half, squeaked by with a 35–29 win over SMU.*

232   After all, he's on a four-year scholarship and I'm sitting here with a one-year contract—*referring to why he never gives plays to a quarterback in tough situations.*

Paul W. "Bear" Bryant

Coach: University of Maryland 1945, University of Kentucky 1946–1953, Texas A&M 1954–1957, University of Alabama 1958–1982. Record: 323-85-17.

233   I'm just a plow hand from Arkansas. But I've learned over the years how to hold a team together—how to lift some men up, how to clamp down on others, until finally they've got one heartbeat together, a team.

234   Bottom. Like your ass. Moro Bottom—*said when someone didn't understand him when he mentioned where he was born. Moro Bottom is in Arkansas.*

235   All I had was football. I hung on as though it was life or death, which it was—*referring to his youth.*

236   No coach has ever won a game by what he knows; it's what his players have learned.

237   It isn't the size of the dog in the fight. It's the size of the fight in the dog.

238   I left Texas A&M because my school called me. Mama called and when Mom calls then you just have to come running—*referring to his alma mater, the University of Alabama.*

239   The first time you quit, it's hard. And the second time, it gets easier. And the third time, you don't even have to think about it.

240   I took off my coat and stomped on it, then I took off my tie and stomped on it. Then, as I was walking up to the microphone, I rolled up my sleeves—*referring to the build up to his first speech as coach of Texas A&M.*

241   They say I teach brutal football but the only thing brutal about football is losing.

242   First there are those who are winners and know they are winners. Then there are those who are losers and know they are losers. Then there are those who are not winners but don't know it. They're the ones for me. They never quit trying. They're the soul of our team.

243   If I'd been one of the players, I might have quit—*comment on how hard he made practice—no water, plenty of body contact.*

244   Eleven men and sic 'em—*his definition of no-substitute football.*

245   I don't think there is any dissension on this team. But if I see anybody out there who's not giving 150 percent, there's going to be some and I'm going to cause it.

246   They're quick and mean and looking for blood. Us? Why, compared to Arkansas, we're Peaceful Valley—*said while coach of Texas A&M.*

247   Hell, no. He'll probably play in the band—*when asked if his son, Paul, Jr., was going to be a football player.*

248   It ain't playing football unless you put your nose where it ain't wanting to go.

249   Believe in the Good Lord.

250   Your parents—always love and obey them.

251   When you have been coaching as long as I have, you get a kick out of watching young men go out into the business or professional world and do well.

252   Gentlemen, a day like this is the reason you're Alabama football players while others are somewhere else. I know it's hot. Hell, I'm hot. I know you're tired. I'm tired, too. I know it's tough. But it's supposed to be.... Believe me, when it gets down to nut-cracking time, when it's tough in the fourth quarter, you'll be glad you didn't quit out here in this heat.

253   If a man's a quitter, I want him to quit in practice, not in a game—*referring to why he made practice so difficult.*

254   There's no sin in not liking to play.

255   If we have an intercepted pass, I threw it. I'm the head coach. If we get a punt blocked, I caused it. A bad practice, a bad game, it's up to the head coach to assume his responsibility.

256   To me, it's time wasted when you sleep past six.

257   The bear finally shook loose and the next thing I knew his muzzle had come off. I felt a burning sensation behind my ear and when I touched it I got a handful of blood. The damned bear bit me. I jumped from the stage and fell into the empty chairs in the front row. Still have the marks on my shins. Then I ran up the aisle and out the theater. When I came around later the man from the circus was gone. I never did get my money. All I got were some scars and a name—*referring to when he wrestled a bear at 14 years old.*

258   Enjoy how warm and soft that little hand you're holding is when you walk across campus, because the memory of it is going to keep you company on the bench on Saturday—*said as a warning not to date girls.*

259   The greatest backs 10, 20, 30 years ago would be great now, too.

260   Don't be a football coach unless you can't live without it.

261   Discipline is not what it used to be.

262   If you're angry, don't take it out on the players.

263   Don't talk too much or too soon.

264   Being number one is like courting a girl. Once you get your hands on her, you don't like to let her go.

265   When I first came to Texas A&M I had been coaching for 12 years and I came here from Kentucky and Mother and I were invited to a party in Dallas at the home of some rich oil man, maybe Clint Murchison. When we were ready to leave, Mary Harmon (his wife) couldn't find her claim check but the fellow we were with said we didn't need it, and he told the girl in the cloakroom she wouldn't have any trouble finding it, "It's the only cloth job there." Now I had been coaching 12 years. The next day I went down to Houston and borrowed some money from Doc Doherty, an Aggie friend of mine, and bought Mother a fur coat.

266   This is strictly, strictly confidential, but if everything went right, what would you think of the possibility of a movie autobiography type of a thing? If this has any possibility, we should do it before John Wayne gets too old because he would probably be the only guy who could do the job—*said after he wrote an autobiography.*

267   Don't give up on ability. I used to be stupid. I'd let some guys go just because we weren't getting along. Find a way to get the talent into the game.

268   Plan for everything. Don't be caught flatfooted.

269   I've had a full life in one respect. But I've had a one-track deal in another respect. My life has been so tied up with football, it has flown by. I wish it wasn't that way, but it has gone by mighty fast. Practice, recruiting and games; there hasn't been anything except football.

270   The second thing I look at in the paper every morning is the stock market tables. First thing is Ann Landers, usually on page six.

271   Don't do a lot of coaching just before the game. If you haven't coached them by 14 minutes to two on Saturday, it's too late then.

272   I've made so many mistakes that if I don't make the same mistake over, we're going to come pretty close to winning.

273   The trouble was, we were too much alike. He wanted basketball number one and I wanted football number one—*referring to Adolph Rupp and the reason Bryant left coaching at the University of Kentucky.*

274   I understand people had heart attacks watching it and one Alabama sportswriter died in the press box right after—*referring to game Alabama lost to Notre Dame after leading three times, 24–23.*

275   The players won in spite of me.

276   I encourage my players to come in and see me if they have a problem. But the young ones, they don't.

277   Here in our area, particularly in Alabama, I think our football players have a far-reaching influence on young people.

278   Don't hide behind anybody or anything in a crisis. They're going to find you anyway.

279   If you go through that door, you're gone—*said to a top A&M player who quit the team in the middle of a workout, as he was walking to gate at end of practice field.*

280   I won't take him back, but I will help him pack—*referring to same player.*

281   What's the matter? Don't you people take football seriously?—*said after making an office call at 7 A.M. to another coach and being told he wasn't in yet.*

282   They just flat whipped our butts in every way known to man—*referring to Orange Bowl loss to Nebraska in 1971.*

283   All I been hearing is Paul Bryant this and Bear Bryant that, 315 this and 315 that—*said at huge testimonial dinner after breaking Alonzo Stagg's record of 314 wins for a coach.*

284   Mother, if I croak now, all you have to do is just lay me out—*said to his wife, at the same dinner, after listening to all the speeches.*

285   I didn't coach until I was 90—*reply when he retired and was asked if he'd achieved all his goals.*

286   I'm a tired old man, but not tired of football.

287   They said it was 75 percent smoking, 20 percent diet and 5 percent booze and other stuff. I wish it had been 75 percent of that booze and other stuff—*reply when asked why he was hospitalized.*

288   Quit coaching? I'd croak in a week.

289   When I take my walk, it's the only time I can smoke without someone lecturing me.

290   I weigh 208 on my trainer's scales and 199 on my wife's. I like my wife's scales.

291   Men, we've got Tennessee right where we want them—*said during halftime speech when his team was down 17–7; it won the game, 27–17.*

292   Alabama quarterbacks don't look like that—*said to a player with a beard, who immediately shaved it off.*

293   We are in direct competition with the pros, make no mistake about that.

294   A champion pays an extra price to be better than everybody else.

295   There is still time. You can still do it, if you believe you can—*said to Texas A&M players losing 12–0 to Rice with three minutes left. Miraculously, Bryant's team won, 20–12.*

296   Damned if I know. I was too busy praying—*reply when asked what happened in the above-mentioned come-from-behind game.*

297   Most games are decided by five or six plays. The secret to winning football is having the right players on the field when those five or six plays happen.

298   I haven't heard that song yet—*said when he kept A&M from coming onto field for game until band played "The Eyes of Texas," delaying kickoff five minutes.*

299   Coach Stagg was the Babe Ruth of college football. To me, he is on a pedestal. In those days he didn't have a large staff. I've heard his wife scouted games for him and both of them mended uniforms. It was a completely different game then.

300   All I know is, if you have on a different colored jersey than me, I want to beat your ass.

301   Losing just makes me get up earlier in the morning and find a way to beat you.

302   A good quick small team can beat a big slow team anytime.

303   Pat, do you want to keep your job? — *to an assistant coach, who said there are no geniuses in coaching.*

304   The Arkansas boy was just running for a touchdown. Osborne was running for his life — *referring to why slow Roddy Osborne, of Texas A&M, tackled faster opponent.*

305   We never had to outbid anyone. We just met the competition — *referring to recruiting.*

306   Every fall when the team reports, I make a speech and I tell the new players to leave those drugs alone, they kill your sex drive. And we've never had a problem.

307   If I can't love them and pat them and brag on them, I don't want them.

308   I want to win it all.

Jerome M. "Jerry" Burns

Coach: University of Iowa 1961–1965, Minnesota Vikings 1986– . Record: 57-55-2.

309   I thought we had it with six minutes to go and a 12-point lead — *said after losing, 44–38, to Washington in overtime.*

310   It's like the guy who's captain of the *Queen Mary*. The captain doesn't run to the boiler room to make sure the boiler is stoked. He's not in the commissary to see if there's enough ice cream. He tries to get the whole thing going and get into port — *referring to the head coach's job.*

311   I can't stand anything that crawls whether it's living or dead.

Hugh Campbell

Coach: Whitworth College 1970–1976, Edmonton Eskimos (CFL) 1977–1982, Los Angeles (USFL) 1983, Houston Oilers 1984–1985. Record: 121-83-5.

312   If I use him too much, I'm taking a big risk of his getting injured and that would be a disaster. Yet, if I hold him out, I'm taking my best offensive weapon out of the game — *referring to Earl Campbell, running back.*

Francis W. "Frank" Cavanaugh

Coach: University of Cincinnati 1898, Holy Cross 1903–1905, Dartmouth 1911–1916, Boston College 1919–1926, Fordham University 1927–1932. Record: 145-48-17.

313   Football should be played to the utmost limits of respectability.

314   Heaphy, how in the name of God are you, a center, ever going to teach football after looking at the game upside down all these years?—*said to Jack Heaphy, a Boston College player, who told Cavanaugh that he, too, wanted to coach a team.*

315   I just couldn't keep out of it. Impossible after teaching so many hundreds of youngsters how to play and fight on the football fields—*reply when asked about his reason for accepting a commission as a major in the US Army during World War I.*

316   I hope the world won't be foolish enough to get into this kind of mess again, but if it does, I'd want my sons to do exactly as I have, without hesitation and without whimpering—*all of Cavanaugh's nine children, six boys and three girls, were in the military during World War II.*

317   I insisted that they keep fit, and to practice what I preached I had to keep fit myself.

George "Potsy" Clark

Coach: Michigan State 1920, University of Kansas 1921–1925, Butler 1927–1929, Portsmouth Spartans/Detroit Lions 1931–1936 and 1940 (team moved and changed name after 1933 season), Brooklyn Dodgers 1937–1939, University of Nebraska 1945 and 1948. Record: 109-89-23.

318   You people, you 11 men, are going to stay in this game. The only way any one of you is going to come out is by being carried off on a stretcher—*said to his team in 1932 when it played the Green Bay Packers. The Spartans won, 19–0, and were dubbed "The Iron Men."*

Blanton Collier

Coach: University of Kentucky 1954–1961, Cleveland Browns 1963–1970. Record: 120-74-7.

319   You can accomplish anything you want as long as you don't care who gets the credit for it.

320   Believe in the teachability of the student. Everyone can learn. You just have to find the right way to teach him.

321   Blitzing is no defensive panacea.

322   A good quarterback has the answer to any blitz, just as he should have the answer to any defense if he recognizes it in time.

Al Conover

Coach: Rice University 1972–1975. Record: 15-27-2.

323   I'm going to be a hog farmer. After some of the things I've been through, I regard it as a step up.

James G. "Jimmy" Conzelman

Coach: Rock Island Independents 1922, Milwaukee Badgers 1923–1924, Detroit Panthers 1925–1926, Providence Steamrollers 1927–1930, Washington University (MO) 1934–1939, Chicago Cardinals 1940–1942 and 1946–1948. Record: 88-67-17 (excludes college record).

324   The first requisite of coaching happiness is a job.

325   As a player I got $150 a game and as a player-coach I got $150 a game—*referring to his first coaching job at Rock Island in 1922, when he was 23.*

326   In those days all a football coach needed to get a job was a journeyman's knowledge of the off-tackle play and a yen to kick anyone who happened to be in a crouching position.

327   Either Cicero wasn't ready for me or I wasn't ready for Cicero—*referring to a week's booking as a piano player between seasons.*

328   One of the first things I did when I took over the Cardinals was write a fight song called, "It's in the Cards to Win." Oh, how wrong I was for the first three years.

329   In the silence of a chastened dressing room it makes a hell of a noise—*referring to a slammed door, a door slammed by an angry coach exiting after yelling at his team.*

330   That's the one where the coach stands before the squad sniffling and wiping his eyes, indicating to the boys that, since he may not be with the team the following season because of hitherto undisclosed broken health, he would be grateful for just one more victory. A closing, husky, "God bless you, boys," is considered entirely ethical where a desperate situation, such as a three-touchdown handicap, must be overcome—*referring to a college locker-room pep talk category.*

331   Among the pros, the coach answers to one man, the owner. In college, he does his explaining to hundreds—*referring to alumni.*

332   Football is a handy votive lamp around which all can gather—*referring to alumni.*

333   The alumnus and professional sports fan have some things in common. Both are football's pulmonary arteries, pumping the good red blood of ready cash into a structure that otherwise would languish with financial anemia.

334   I don't miss the college game at all. I like the pro version better.

335   He feels like a scientist who has escaped from classroom routine to a laboratory full of exciting new equipment—*referring to his preference for coaching professional teams.*

336   I have only the most profound admiration for a kid who loves the game so much he is willing, even eager, to absorb its body beatings without the reward of a first-team starting assignment or the soothing syrup of a newspaper headline.

337   I didn't have much faith in the future of pro football—*referring to why he left the sport to become an executive.*

Donald D. "Don" Coryell

Coach: Wenatchee Valley Junior College 1955, Whittier College 1957–1959, San Diego State 1961–1972, St. Louis Cardinals 1973–1978, San Diego Chargers 1978–1986. Record: 245-107-5.

338   You kick the ball and get off the field—*said to Rolf Benirschke, who wore external pouch because part of colon had been removed, who wanted to play football for the Chargers in 1980.*

339   I know kids who'd rather go to USC or Notre Dame and sit on the bench than play regularly elsewhere. They can say they played for Notre Dame and that's prestige.

340 I'm not a genius. Sometimes I can't even spell my name.

341 Where's he play?—*said when asked his opinion of the Ayatollah Khomeini.*

342 Don't you think it would be wonderful if we could have Popsicles during practice?

343 We've got to leave two days before the game.... We've got to, otherwise our bodies aren't going to be there, they're going to be thinking a different time.

Herbert O. "Fritz" Crisler

Coach: University of Minnesota 1930–1931, Princeton 1932–1937, University of Michigan 1938–1947. Record: 116-32-9.

344 Gentlemen, you have 60 minutes for redemption and a lifetime for regret—*said to Michigan players before Rose Bowl game.*

345 He ran it just like I diagrammed it—*said of play by Tom Harmon. Wolverines on their 37-yard line. Harmon started right on end run, saw tacklers, ran towards left side, then ran backwards until he had shed enough University of Pennsylvania tacklers and picked up enough Michigan blockers to start up the right sideline again. He eluded the remaining Quaker defense and raced uncontested the last 50 yards, putting team on top 13–3. Officially a 63-yard touchdown, but he ran more than 100 yards.*

346 I know Tom too well. I know what he has always done when the pressure was on him. I've seen his cocksureness and tremendous physical strength and I just won't believe he's through—*said at special Mass for Tom Harmon at student chapel at University of Michigan in April 1943, after he bailed out of plane gone out of control during storm while flying over Brazil and his chute didn't open. (His parachute got caught in a tree.) After six days of travel in the jungle he was found by an Indian. Said Harmon, "The only things that saved me were a deep religious conviction and a pair of strong legs. If it wasn't for the superb conditioning I received at Michigan, I couldn't have made it."*

347 Offense is poise, defense is frenzy.

348 It's almost impossible to go the whole season and not be scored on—*said after 1933 team's eighth game, when Rutgers became the first opponent that season to score against Princeton.*

349   Our plan is simple, theirs, one of desperation—*referring to the fear other teams had at playing virtually unbeatable Michigan.*

350   The substitution rule was changed in 1941. Until that time players could not reenter a game in the same quarter they had left. The restriction was removed, and all that remained was the provision allowing a player to enter the game at any time the clock was stopped. Those three little words "at any time" gave me the opportunity of using separate teams for offense and defense—*referring to the start of the two-platoon system.*

351   My last official act at Minnesota was an effort to entice Bernie Bierman to leave Tulane and cast his lot with his alma mater. We met in the Palmer House in Chicago where for two hours I reviewed the many advantages and bright future at Minnesota. Bernie was never known to be loquacious, so I finally suggested, "Bernie, you probably have some questions you would like to raise about a contract." His only response was, "Where do I sign?" Little did I suspect that that act would haunt me in later years.

352   I am happy to be coming to Princeton and I want you people to know that I would rather lose than win with one player with the taint of proselytism upon him!—*said when he was drunk.*

353   What should I do to keep the press happy? Throw banquets, come up to New York frequently to visit them, just what?

354   I want all you fellows to write your alibis now, explaining how you happened to lose this game. Our alumni will want to know—*said during halftime of a game, after Crisler distributed papers and pencils to a team that was playing poorly against underdog Yale—Michigan ultimately won.*

355   The coach who draws diagrams full of confusing X's and arrows, and who spouts a lot of double-talk, is a phony.

356   When the other fellow has $1,000 and you have a dime is the time to gamble.

357   After I'd thrown maybe a dozen pitches, Walsh came out to the mound, lugging shin guards, chest protector and mask. Here, put these on before you get killed, he said. So ended any hopes that I had of playing professional baseball—*describing tryout with 1920 White Sox—Ed Walsh, pitcher.*

358   I would not risk picking a winner. A break will probably decide.

James H. "Jim" Crowley

Coach: Michigan State 1929–1932, Fordham University 1933–1941, Chicago Rockets (AALF) 1947. Record: 79-34-10.

359   If we lose, I'll not go across the field and shake his hand.

360   I sleep all right at night and in the morning, but in the afternoon I toss and turn something awful.

Hugh "Duffy" Daugherty

Coach: Michigan State 1954–1972. Record: 109-69-5.

361   The secret of this team is that our good sophomores and juniors haven't had the full benefit of my coaching experience.

362   I'm not very quick-witted and it takes me awhile to find out what's going on — *referring to being called "the best fourth quarter coach in the country."*

363   When you're playing for the national championship, it's not a matter of life or death. It's more important than that.

364   You'll notice I didn't say which way — *said when his opponent scored a touchdown by intercepting a pass after Daugherty said, "Here's a play that will go all the way."*

365   Kids 18 and 19 have to feel you are approachable.

366   When you're winning, everybody thinks the happy, informal approach is wonderful. When you're losing, they think you're not serious enough.

367   I've been asked to make a speech about my football team. My football team that just won nine games. My football team that just won the Rose Bowl. My football team that — I'm sorry, I forgot this wasn't my football team. It really belongs to you. Last year when we won only three and lost five, that was my football team.

368   Let's not be sacrilegious. Let's say Gipp was reaching down — *said during halftime of a game against Notre Dame, when Daugherty's center said some invisible hand was affecting the movement of the ball and another player replied, "Maybe Gipp was reaching up."*

369   Most football games aren't won on the field. They are won from December to September, when the recruiting is done. Eighty percent of a winning team is material. Ten percent is luck. Our biggest job is getting the boys. The thing we do least at Michigan State is coach.

370   Believe me, there are no geniuses in coaching. We all know what the other fellow's got.

371   What it comes down to is, who's got the better players and how badly do they want to play? Today there is so much player talent that the team that gets keyed higher mentally each Saturday comes out the winner.

372   Some people say football is a contact sport. Hell, it's a collision sport. Dancing is a contact sport.

373   We coaches steal from each other. We take everything that isn't nailed down. If it's nailed down, we go get a claw hammer. In the old days we stole plays and formations. Now we steal words and organizational techniques. We don't tell a halfback, "Run like hell to that side of the field." We tell him, "Flare left." When a coach is successful, others copy him. This isn't just football. It's an industry, too.

374   An ordinary student who is an extraordinary athlete deserves every chance for an education. There are lots of ordinary students who didn't play football.

375   As for Phi Beta Kappas, I could have been one myself if I had made better grades.

376   Character is built at home and in the church.

377   The trouble with Michigan State fans is that they get carried away by my enthusiasm.

378   I don't mind the guy who wrote me to say what a bum coach I am. But I did object to the way the post office delivered it. It arrived on my desk in the usual time. The only address on it was, "To Duffy the Dope."

379   Yes, it's on the radio and television here. They must be hard up for news—*said after he signed a five-year coaching contract giving him tenure and the security of a can't-be-fired clause.*

380   It's an old gag but this is a game of inches, just like baseball.

381   My only feeling about superstition is that it's unlucky to be behind at the end of a game.

382   Only three things can happen when you put the ball up in the air and two of them are bad.

383   This is the only place I know where windows clean people—*said after losing at the racetrack.*

384   You never know what you're going to do until the situation arises.

385   Life without work is insipid and life without fun and relaxation is deadening.

Robert S. "Bob" Devaney

Coach: University of Wyoming 1957–1961, University of Nebraska 1962–1972. Record: 136-30-7.

386   We're going for a touchdown. No field goals, no ties.

387   I had a friend with a lifetime contract. After two bad years the university president called him into his office and pronounced him dead.

388   I don't expect to win enough games to be put on NCAA probation. I just want to win enough to warrant an investigation.

389   If your offense hangs onto the football, the other team cannot score.

390   The prospect enrolled at the University of Missouri. His mother, however, decided to go back to college. She, of course, enrolled at Nebraska.

391   Not even the Pope would vote Notre Dame number one—*said in 1970.*

392   And any time you can save a person, you've got to try. If we had dropped him from the team, we'd have ruined his life. He hadn't any way of making real money at the time other than what he did on the football field—*said of '72 Heisman Trophy winner, Johnny Rodgers, placed on probation after gas station holdup.*

393   You're getting a great player, but he's going to take up 80 percent of your time—*said to Coach Marv Levy, Montreal Alouettes, Canadian Football League, after Johnny Rodgers, a troublemaker, joined team. Five years later, Levy saw Devaney and replied, "You were wrong. He took up 95 percent."*

Daniel J. "Dan" Devine

Coach: Arizona State 1955–1957, Missouri 1958–1970, Green Bay Packers 1971–1974, Notre Dame 1975–1980. Record: 197-85-13.

394   There is a tradition of winning here. That may not seem like an important factor, but I think it is — *said when he joined Notre Dame.*

395   In my younger days I would have felt compelled to make changes just to show I was in charge. I don't have to do that now.

Paul F. Dietzel

Coach: LSU 1955–1961, Army 1962–1965, University of South Carolina 1966–1974. Record: 109-95-5.

396   They didn't run off the field, they floated.

397   You've got to be good but you've got to be lucky, too.

Michael K. "Mike" Ditka

Coach: Chicago Bears 1982– . Record: 84-45.

398   There are teams that are fair-haired and some that aren't fair-haired. There are teams named Smith and some named Grabowski. We're Grabowskis.

399   You're only as good as your last game and our last game wasn't very good.

400   If we're starting to pay football players $1.2 million a year, this game is dead — *said after Chicago's linebacker, William Marshall, signed a five-year, $6 million free-agent offer sheet with rival Washington.*

401   I believe everyone has a destiny in life and mine is with the Chicago Bears.

402   Inside the ten you field nothing, and here's why: most kicks bouncing inside the ten will find their way into the end zone.

403   You make up all sorts of rules and it just creates rebellion.

404   If you're not in the parade, you watch the parade—that's life.

405   Always, when things don't go well, the finger's pointed at me. I guess I'm the finger guy.

406   Put a chip on your shoulder in July and keep it there until January—*referring to how to win the Super Bowl.*

407   We had something to prove. All we proved is we won one game.

408   She don't dance on this field—*referring to prima donnas.*

409   There's nobody I wouldn't replace.

410   How tough was Aliquippa? Our definition of quick hands was a guy who could steal hubcaps off a car that was moving—*comment on his hometown in Pennsylvania.*

411   I want my coaches to be coaches and teachers. I don't particularly want them to be a father.

412   I feel sorry for assistant coaches in pro football because I don't think they get the recognition they deserve or the respect they deserve or the money they deserve.

413   I don't believe in changing. You lose a few games and what am I going to do? Fire the assistants?

414   Temper has hurt a lot of coaches.

415   A lot of people were surprised I even had a heart—*reply to question about what he had learned from his heart attack.*

416   You're not going to see me anymore like you ever saw me before—*said after heart attack.*

417   I can't control what happens on the field. Sometimes I think I can, but I can't.

418   I can't walk away from something I've done for 28 years—*referring to a question about quitting after his heart attack.*

419   It becomes more than a game because it's your life. You get wrapped up in it. You get wrapped up in the winning and losing and wrapped up in the fans, the disappointments and the joys. You hear people time and time again saying, "I can't tell you how proud we were." Or "I can't tell you how disappointed we were." You realize a big part of their lives revolves around what happens every Sunday afternoon. Maybe it shouldn't be that way, but it is that way.

420 The key to success in life is opportunity and what you do with it.

421 Anything can be a factor if you want it to be a factor. It can also be a cop-out.

422 I don't want anybody smiling around here. We're getting ready to go to war.

423 I'm an adult. I have a right to drink. That's my business if I want to do it. But I don't have a right to drink and drive—*said after conviction for drunken driving.*

424 I'm not exactly the image of an NFL coach. I'm not over there on the sidelines, wearing glasses, my arms folded, looking studious, am I?

425 What the heck, if a guy is a minute late to a meeting well, then, maybe we'll go a minute longer.

426 My job is to pat on the back and kick in the butt.

427 Friends are hard to find; you can find a wife anywhere.

428 This guy has one arm and one leg, but he shouldn't be on the goddamn football field if he doesn't want to get hit—*telling team to get Tom Dempsey, born with withered arm and a right foot that doesn't go much beyond the ankle. The rest of his foot is made out of lead.*

429 I think I broke my hand—*said after pounding equipment locker after Bears lost to Baltimore in overtime in '83.*

430 The Old Man throws quarters around like manhole covers—*referring to the cheapness of George Halas.*

431 I had to look around and see if it was anybody from our bench—*said after someone ran naked onto the field during an exhibition game.*

432 I can tell the players are getting ready when they gripe and complain and get mad at me.

433 He's going to look good in that navy blue uniform, or two uniforms, whatever it takes—*said when the Bears got 300-pound-plus William "Refrigerator" Perry.*

434 He's running twice a day. From the refrigerator to the bathroom—*comment about Perry.*

435 Life is here to use, not abuse.

436 This was Seeing-Eye dog weather—*referring to December 31, 1988, playoff game against the Eagles, played in heavy fog.*

437   I guess you could call him an unsung hero, but he's pretty sung now—*referring to Dennis Gentry.*

438   The big plays will happen as often by improvisation as by design.

439   You take what the defense gives you.

440   You're not going to win football games tricking people. The more new plays you try, the more you are only fooling yourself.

441   What you do in life by yourself doesn't mean as much as what you accomplish with a group of people.

442   Everybody asks me, "What kind of relationship do you have with Jim McMahon?" I say it's strange and wonderful. He's strange and I'm wonderful.

443   They tell me about 600-pound marlin off Hawaii, of fighting them for ten hours. That's nonsense. Why, that's two rounds of golf right there.

444   That was global. This is galaxy—*describing the importance of his next game, after stating the outcome of his previous game would have global significance.*

445   Last year was last year. Doesn't mean a thing.

446   In baseball, if you get a hit one out of every two at bats, you're going to be all-world. In football, you do it right one out of two times and you're going to get beat. The championship level for football falls around 80 percent.

447   If you take the time a player is truly in motion in a game, put the clock on it, I think the total action time is somewhere around four minutes and 10 seconds. That's not a lot to ask for a player's utmost concentration.

448   You've got to build up the "us against them" thing.

449   I don't look at statistics. Do you win or do you lose?

450   You have to try to get their weaker personnel on your stronger personnel and you do that by changing formations and moving around.

451   If we approached it like a war, it would probably be better for us. We'd have fewer guys patting each other on the fanny all the time.

452   If you have all the experience in the world and line up against somebody with more physical ability, you'll get beat.

453   If you put loyalty ahead of talent you've got some problems. If we were 0–6, who'd be loyal to me?

454   Success is about having and excellence is about being. Success is about having money and fame and endorsements. But excellence is being the very best you can be all the time.

455   The hard part is not what's past, it's what's coming.

456   What I told them today is, the most important thing in life, football, business and success is all a matter of attitude. You are what you think you are.

457   Indoor domes should be used for roller rinks. Football was meant to be played outside on grass.

458   I owe my whole life to football.

Gilmour Dobie

Coach: North Dakota State 1906–1907, University of Washington 1908–1916, Navy 1917–1919, Cornell 1920–1935, Boston College 1936–1938. Record: 180-45-15.

459   Can't you see the opportunity? We might have to play in conditions like this — *said to Boston College players who quit workout in midst of hurricane with branches and wooden seats flying about.*

460   Many a tomato has been made to look like a peach through the pressure of publicity.

461   The power of of ballyhoo may make a few men greater but often has the tendency to make many of them light-headed.

462   Tooting one's own horn is frowned upon in sportsmanship, and there is no reason why excessive verbal splurging about a football player should not merit equal disapproval in the eyes of the public.

463   After all, I'm just the coach — *after his team, Cornell, lost to Princeton, 54–0, in 1935.*

464   You kick off here. *(Points to 40-yard line.)* There is where you sit when you're not playing. *(Walks to bench.)* Here is where you'll be all afternoon with your backs to the wall. *(Walks to 10-yard line.)*

465   Yeah, it was a good game as long as you had your fourth team in there — *said to Red Blaik, Dartmouth coach, after Cornell's 41–6 loss.*

466   You can't win games with Phi Beta Kappas.

467   No little peasant is going to improve on my plays and get away with it—*said to receiver who caught touchdown pass in "wrong place"—according to diagrammed plans—in the end zone.*

468   When I'm traveling I ask farm boys how to get to a certain place. If they point with their finger, I move on. If they pick up the plow and point with it, I stop and sell them on the University of Minnesota—*said while assistant coach at Minnesota.*

469   Some people seem to have the idea that I object to a boy's coming to college and studying. Let me say that I think this is the only reason a boy should come to college and if football interferes with his studies he should drop football.

470   Young man, you don't know what sorrow is—wait till next year—*reply to a member of his team, who said he was sorry after losing 49–0.*

471   The control of the team should be in the hands of the coach who is responsible and not shifted to the shoulders of the captain, who under the rules has quite enough duties to perform on the field.

472   I suppose you are proud of that tackle. If his arm had come off, they had six points—*said to last defender before the goal line, who caught the ball carrier by the wrist and swung him around a few times to bring him down.*

473   Let me congratulate you fellows on being good losers. Good? Hell, you were perfect.

474   They get to the tacklers too soon—*referring to the problem with his backs.*

Robert L. "Bobby" Dodd

Coach: Georgia Tech 1945–1966. Record: 165-64-8.

475   After the game, we were both crying—*referring to the emotions of parent and child after the University of Florida, quarterbacked by Dodd's son, beat Georgia Tech, 18–17.*

476   I had the kind of boys whom I knew wouldn't violate my trust. They didn't—*referring to very few rules he imposed upon his players when they went to New Orleans for the Sugar Bowl.*

477   You want to get interested in something, then you gamble for more money than you have in the bank — *referring to an addiction to gambling on golf, cured in the 1940s.*

478   A man who had played regularly for me never had to come out for spring practice the following year. He didn't need it.

479   You have to listen to your assistant coaches. They're young and aggressive and always look for ways to improve.

480   The key to my training was to let the boys off as much as possible.

481   Most coaches get their theories from the people they played for or coached under.

482   It's tragic to see the situation football coaches get into when they start losing. They can be hated by the student body and finally browbeaten under the terrific pressure to do anything.

483   I never believed smoking hurt a player as much as some coaches did.

484   There is no point in rough scrimmages before a bowl game. Your top players learn nothing playing against the third team and you risk injury.

485   I used the quick kick a lot and still believe in it. Coaches are stupid not to use it. There's no chance of a runback and it puts the opponent deep in its territory where it may make a mistake and give you an easy touchdown.

486   You have to brainwash your players.

487   Men, the odds makers have Auburn as a six-point favorite over us here on our home field. I think they're right — *said before a game Georgia Tech won, 23–14.*

488   I talk at a lot of banquets these days — *said after his retirement.*

489   College football can be a beautiful thing.

Vincent J. "Vince" Dooley

Coach: University of Georgia 1964–1988. Record: 201-77-10.

490   Winning made me happy but I didn't feel like celebrating — *referring to victory over North Carolina, coached by his brother, Bill.*

491   I don't think the way you are is the way you always will be.

492   You have the responsibility of a position. It gives you an incentive for control.

493   Someone once told me, "Marry somebody who will bring you up to their level. Not someone who will bring you down." I did.

494   There are many reasons why I have decided to remain at Georgia. I've been here 17 years, coached 17 football teams and have built too many ties and friendships over the years to make the change now. I have spent 17 years with the Georgia people and in the final analysis I just couldn't leave — *said when he turned down offer to coach Auburn.*

495   There were too many things left undone here at Georgia. It's my program.

496   We seem to find some way, somehow, to win. This team hangs in there, gnaws at people, and if one aspect of our game is having a bad day, then another phase will pick us up.

497   Even if I went to open-heart surgery somewhere down the road, where all the valves were clogged, then I'll have open-heart surgery and I'll come back and coach ten more years like Bo Schembechler. And then I'll get another open-heart surgery and I'll be ready to start again — *said after he'd been in the hospital the third time to have his partially blocked arteries cleared through the insertion of a balloon.*

Pat Dye

Coach: East Carolina 1974–1979, University of Wyoming 1980, Auburn 1981– . Record: 135-48-3.

498   There weren't no place out there for women and children.

R. LaVell Edwards

Coach: Brigham Young University 1972– . Record: 165-56-1.

499   For a coach, it makes it tough to recruit. You're always having to project which players will be available when — *referring to fact that Mormons at BYU might decide to take a year off to act as missionaries.*

500   We need a big, strong 240-pound lineman a lot more than the Lord needs a big fat missionary—*said to a Morman football player at BYU who was thinking about interrupting college to proselytize.*

501   Relieved—*reply when asked how he felt when BYU was ranked number one by both UPI and AP in 1984.*

502   A passing game puts a lot more pressure on your defense because you don't keep the ball for long blocks of time.

503   We throw a lot of short passes to our running backs and we get a few yards a very high percentage of the time. Our short pass is almost like a regular halfback dive on a running team.

504   Patience is being able to read the defensive man and be a protector, not an aggressor.

505   When faking, the best fake a back can give is to run as hard as possible. If a running back is tackled as he fakes carrying the football, then he knows that he has done a good job.

506   The longer I am in coaching, the more I am convinced that there is no one best way to coach or to teach a basic technique.

507   Coaching styles can vary from being very autocratic to being very low-key and group-oriented. However in all cases there can only be one boss, the head coach.

508   People say I'm not a happy man. I am. It's just that sometimes I forget to tell my face.

509   The ability to recruit outstanding athletes is the single most important phase of a college football program.

510   Football coaches are not tenured as regular faculty members. Being untenured creates the situation that winning is a must, and, in many cases, coaches are forced to win at any cost. This, in turn, leads to such problems as illegal recruiting, altered transcripts and under-the-table payments to many of our college athletes. Until coaches have the chance to be tenured and gain some type of protection and security for their families, many of these problems will continue to exist.

511   A vicious cycle now exists when the football program needs more money so that great players can be recruited, so that the stands can be filled, so that we can win more games, so that we can generate more interest and excitement, so that more fans will fill the stadium, so that we can generate more money, etc., etc., etc. This need for more revenue puts even greater pressure on football coaches to win.

512   Coaches must remember that their first responsibility is for the academic success—not athletic success—of the student/athletes they have recruited.

513   I'd rather lose and live in Provo than win and live in Laramie—*said after playing in Wyoming during snowstorm.*

514   It is my belief that teams are controlled better by attitudes than by rules.

515   Coaches need to maintain a proper perspective on the role and value of athletics in the lives of young men. It should never come to the point that winning at any cost replaces the building of good character traits.

516   Coaching does and will always win ball games. I am talking about game day coaching. The anticipations and adjustments that coaches make on game day often will make the difference in the outcome of a close contest.

517   Football is a great game.

518   I am convinced that championships are won with defense.

519   The better a team becomes at throwing the football, the better success they will have at running the football, simply because the defense has geared their defenses to stop the pass. This opens up more opportunities for running the ball.

520   Football players are not only bigger, taller and heavier than before, they are also stronger and quicker than at any point in the history of football.

521   Practice, practice and more practice should be the standard rule.

522   The teams that execute best are the teams that usually win.

523   If they don't win, they don't stay long—*referring to coaches.*

524   If a coach is willing to accept the plaudits of success, he likewise must accept the responsibility for defeat.

525   One of the problems in athletics is the tendency for everything to get out of proper perspective.

526   Having to tell people, "No." Telling a player he's not starting. Or telling a kid who would love to come to BYU and who ought to be here that we just don't have a scholarship for him—*referring to the dislikes of his job.*

527   The thing that bothers me more than any one thing are those kids who don't go to class and work toward graduation. It's almost like they think football is going to go on forever and they don't want to face up to reality that someday it's going to come to an end.

528   To me, that's the most incredible thing—*referring to growing up as one of 14 children in a house with one bathroom.*

529   Cold milk—*reply when asked for his favorite drink.*

530   When Patti's lucky outfit wears out—*reply when asked when he'd quit coaching. Patti is his wife.*

Ray Eliot

Coach: Illinois College 1933–1936, University of Illinois 1942–1959. Record: 102-82-13.

531   When I saw those two bodies coming close together, I really wondered what I was going to say to Eddie's mother at the funeral.

532   I have a bust of Lincoln on my desk and every time the going gets rough for me and I sit at that desk, he looks at me with a twinkle in his eye and he tells me something. You know what he tells me? He says, "Ray, remember now, I tried 27 times to be elected to public office. Twenty-seven times I tried to be something. And I failed 25 times." Did you ever stop to think of that guy at the end of the fifth time he failed. Why, he couldn't have been our president.

533   You who lack the heart, you who have lost the spirit and hope, you who have lost self-confidence—you are dead, sir. You are done.

534   When you can get the boys in the proper state of mind, you've got a winner.

535   All right, you guys, if you score from there, I'll buy the milk shakes—*said to team getting ball on one-yard line in practice game.*

Peter R. "Pete" Elliot

Coach: University of Nebraska 1956, University of California 1957–1959, University of Illinois 1960–1966, University of Miami (FL) 1973–1974. Record: 56-72-1.

536   I asked him if he was in the top half of his class academically. He said, "No sir, I'm one of those who make the top half possible."

Edward J. "Eddie" Erdelatz

Coach: Navy 1950–1958, Oakland Raiders 1960–1961. Record: 56-36-8.

537   Hard work. Hard, frustrating work—*reply when asked for the secret of his success.*

538   Everything at Annapolis is great. Now, do you want to talk to me off the record—*reply when a reporter asked him to comment, on the record, about the problems of coaching at Annapolis.*

539   It's a silent prayer because we have Jewish, Protestant and Catholic players. Me? I pray that nobody gets hurt—*referring to the two minutes of time for silent prayer he held just before game time.*

540   Navy is a team called Desire.

541   I got them from the hard pillows in my dormitory—*referring to his cauliflower ears, a result of refusing to wear a helmet while playing college football.*

542   I never thought the so-called skull sessions did much good. If you talk to the ends, the tackles doze off and if you talk to the tackles, the ends lose interest.

Forrest Evashevski

Coach: Hamilton (NY) 1941, Washington State 1950–1951, University of Iowa 1952–1960. Record: 68-35-6.

543   No player who ever played for me laid down conditions. He played only under my terms.

544   The psychological aspects of football are invariably puzzling.

545   There are some players who can sing songs in the shower before a game. All I say is bless them for whatever it is they have to do to prepare for a game as long as they can execute for you.

546   Score if you can, but don't pass.

Wilbur C. "Weeb" Ewbank

Coach: University of Washington (MO) 1947–1948, Baltimore Colts 1954–1962, New York Jets 1963–1973. Record: 148-134-7.

547   It was a bad season, but it was a great game—*said of Jets' 31–20 win against the Rams in 1970, when the Jets were 4 and 10.*

548   He signed that contract sitting at the desk in my office. He had that Mohawk haircut and he was stripped to the waist and he was wearing leather pants and a derby hat with a feather in it. It must have been what the sale of Manhattan looked like—*referring to signing of John Riggins.*

549   I guess it won't look bad when he puts his helmet on—*said when John Riggins reported to Jets' training camp with Mohawk haircut and gold pearl in earlobe.*

550   Some people judge the strictness of a coach on how loudly he yells at his players on the practice field. I, for one, do not.

551   Teaching and discipline are a matter of respect based on mutual understanding, not on antagonism.

552   I believe coaching, more than anything else, is teaching, and that's why I love it so.

553   The reasoning behind any rule you impose as a coach is, "Will it help the team to win?" If it is not geared to this end, it has no place on a team.

554   Well, that's one good thing about this place. If they want it, it's right here on campus. They don't have to go driving into New York at all hours for it. And you know the ones that are going to get it are going to get it somehow—*said in '68 when Jets trained at Hofstra University in Hempstead, LI, about 30 miles from New York, where there were pretty coeds.*

555   Your game plan is just a description of your strength and weaknesses and those of your opponent. It breaks down into which plays you think you can use most effectively against the opposition. If your scouting is good and your analysis of the reports is accurate, you can come up with a good game plan. If you stick to that game plan, execute the plays properly and avoid mistakes, chances are you will win the game.

556   It took me 40 years to collect this playbook of mine but it doesn't mean a damn thing if you don't have the people to put it to use.

557   He has size, quickness, a wonderful arm, a quick delivery, courage and the ability to make the big play. We say in the pros that it takes three or more years to make a quarterback out of a college boy, but it won't take that long for Joe. There are veteran pros who can't react the way he does right now. He has reactions a lot of quarterbacks could never learn—*referring to Joe Namath.*

558   I really wish Joe hadn't said that. Actually we all knew we would win, we just didn't want the Colts to know—*referring to pre-'68 Super Bowl comment made by Joe Namath, "We'll win. I guarantee it."*

559   Don't worry about it. You're my quarterback again next week—*said to Johnny Unitas after he came in game as a substitute quarterback and the other team scored 38 more points to win.*

560   Applaud!—*reply to a rookie who, during practice, asked, "What do I do now, coach?" after numerous unsuccessful attempts to stop a star runner.*

561   Pass defense is a coordination between the rush and the coverage. The linemen must pressure the passer, so the cornerbacks' job isn't so tough, but you can't have the rush unless the coverage is there, too. If the backs are laying too loose, the quarterback can throw quick passes for yardage and he isn't affected by the rush that much.

562   You show me a man who shoots a good game of golf and I'll bet he neglects his business or someone else does his work for him. I don't have time for golf.

563   Scatter guys. They keep scattering around out there until one day they don't get up—*referring to quarterbacks who are freewheeling scramblers instead of operating from the blocking pocket.*

564   Some coaches are fortunate in that they inherit teams that are instant winners. I was fortunate enough to have a team that had the potential to grow into a winner—*referring to when he took over as coach of the Colts.*

565   Winning a championship one year does not guarantee that you are going to repeat the following year. It does not even guarantee you will be in contention.

566   Champions are made by talent, hard work and a little luck.

567   I hate those things. I like a writer to interview me with a pad and pencil, so I can see what he's doing. Those tape recorders pick up every damn word you say.

568   One year Jim Parker has a job selling cemetery lots. He kept pestering Big Daddy about them and finally Big Daddy couldn't stand it anymore. "OK," he said, "gimme two in the shade"—*Big Daddy Lipscomb, member of the Colts.*

569   You just have to be there when the keel is laid, not when the ship is launched—*referring to sex and the birth of a child.*

570   The way to attack a zone is to hit what we call the seams of the zone, its dead spots. Imagine pieces of cloth sewn together so that you have several sections. The sewn spots, or seams, are not in any of the sections. So it is with a zone defense. There are dead spots, which are the areas not quite covered by any of the defensive men—areas between the defenders.

571   We had three teams back then. We had today's team on the field, yesterday's team checking out and tomorrow's team driving in—*referring to high turnover during his first few Jets training camps.*

572   These games are for training. Don't take them seriously. We'll try to win but we also will try to give all of the young men in uniform a chance to win jobs—*referring to exhibition games.*

573   He tackles everybody and then throws them away until he comes to the one with the ball—*referring to "Big Daddy" Lipscomb.*

574   I've always read every letter I ever got, for that reason, because of that one-in-a-thousand shot that comes in—*referring to fact that he learned about Johnny Unitas from a letter written by a fan.*

575   Every time you lose a coach to some other team, there goes another playbook.

576   I didn't hire a coach from Johns Hopkins. I hired a coach who knows football—*reply to criticism of hiring an assistant from a small school.*

Raymond "Ray" Flaherty

Coach: Gonzaga University 1930, Boston/Washington Redskins 1936–1942 (team moved after 1936 season), New York Yankees 1946–1948, Chicago Hornets 1949. Record: 82-44-5.

577   If that guy has got a conscience, he'll never have another good night's sleep as long as he lives—*referring to referee who made controversial call that cost his team 1939 NFL championship.*

578   I want you to hit him square in the eye with the ball—*said to quarterback Sammy Baugh, who replied, "Sure, coach. One thing, coach— which eye?"*

Thomas R. "Tom" Flores

Coach: Oakland/Los Angeles Raiders 1979–1987 (team moved after '81 season). Record: 91-56.

579   It was at halftime early in the season and we went to the blackboards. Each coach went over with his people what he wanted done—the adjustments that had to be made for the second half. Everyone attended to business and before we knew it, halftime was over. This one veteran we had just traded for came up to me shaking his head. "Where I came from we spent the whole time in the locker room getting our asses chewed out. Here, we've spent the time figuring out how to win."

580   We are one of the very few teams that has the quarterback call his own plays. Throughout the week we'll have quarterback meetings and go over every situation we think is possible—short yardage, goal line, inside the 20, plays against the nickel defense, first down plays, running plays. As a result, our quarterbacks call about 75 percent of their own plays. We send in all short yardage and goal line plays and will always call the first play in a series and sometimes a special play at a certain point on the field.

581   It's good to play games where everything comes down to the wire.

582   We're inheriting quarterbacks that have never called a play in their lives. It goes all the way back to high school.

583   I'm a very strong believer in execution rather than too much deception.

584   A lot of times a player who doesn't have the understanding and the player who just can't do the job look the same. Those that learn quickly and study—repetition is very important to the process—are usually the ones who will rise to the top and make your team.

Hayden Fry

Coach: Southern Methodist 1962–1972, North Texas State 1973–1978, University of Iowa 1979– . Record: 171-135-8.

585   I'm the oratorial equivalent of a blocked punt.

Alonzo S. "Jake" Gaither

Coach: Florida A&M 1945–1969. Record: 203-36-4.

586   Excuses are no good. Your friends don't need them and your enemies won't believe them. So why make them?

587   I just organize. Just give me credit for selecting good assistants.

588   I want my boys to be agile, mobile and hostile.

589   I don't like good-natured football players. We don't want anybody running over others and then apologizing. Mow him down, then stand over him and yell, "I'll eat you up." Make him wish he had never been born.

590   A lot of coaches disagree, but I believe in the old-time pep talk. I belong to the school of Knute Rockne.

591   I made it a habit never to leave the field with a boy feeling that I was mad at him. Before I left the field, I'd pat him on the shoulder and say, "Don't think I got anything against you. I'm chewing you out for your own good. You're still my boy." That means a lot to that kid. If you don't do something like that to the boy, when he comes to practice the next day, he's got a chip on his shoulder—he figures Coach is mad at him and he's still in the doghouse. He'll sulk and you won't get the best work out of him. But if you let him know that you'll forgive him—just don't make that mistake again—the guy will come back with plenty of enthusiasm, believing "I'm still Coach's boy."

592   I love America. Oh, they tell me that my home is in Africa. But I want to tell you one thing: I'm not a bit homesick.

593   You need to go to a black school to learn something about the people you got to live and die with—*said while recruiting students to his all-black university.*

594   I always sang the blues and I did it on purpose. Regardless of what I had at the beginning of the season, I'd say, "Well, we got a tough job, we lost so many key men, we got inexperienced kids, we just hope we can win more than we lose." All right, as the season goes along and we win the first game, they say, "He must have done a helluva job. He told us he didn't have anything to start with." You win the second game and they say, "You know, that guy is a helluva coach out there. He started with nothing." And if you have a good season, they'll say, "Man, he did a helluva job." If you lose a game, they say, "Coach told you out front not to expect too much." Ain't no way in the world you can lose.

595   Dear Father, we're not asking for victory, but only that the best team wins—*prayer said before game.*

596   They say, "Coach, you're old fashioned. You're square. Don't you know there is no such thing as right and wrong? What might be right today may be wrong tomorrow. Right and wrong are relative terms—they change." Don't kid yourself. There are certain eternal truths that never change. They were true two thousand years ago and they'll be true two thousand years hence: truth, honesty, integrity, loyalty, humbleness, love thy father and thy mother, decency. They never change—don't kid yourself. Do the things that you know to be right and refuse to do the things that you know to be wrong.

597   I find this: so many times youngsters want to be told. They'll go just as far as you'll let them. But they respond to reasoning. They know they're wrong and if you approach them in the right way, they'll do right.

598   They talk about what I have given football. No, it's the opposite, it's what football has given me. I can never repay the game of football for the fine things that football has been to me.

599   The hardest thing in the world for me to do was to make a will.

600   He was a fine kicker, and we lost a couple of games after he left that we could have won if he had been kicking for us. But when he would sit in the school cafeteria, a small group of our students, who are militants, would stand over him and say, "Now what are we going to do with him?" Finally, the kid couldn't take anymore and he went home—*referring to the first and only Caucasian student/football player at Gaither's school.*

601   It'll be a long time, if ever, before black schools will get good white athletes. If he's good, the white schools will want him.

602   The urge for power is as great as the urge for sex.

603   It's bad coaching to blame your boys for losing a ball game, even if it's true.

604   I say, "Buddy, you take orders from me." I don't take orders from him. I tell them I don't want it. If they ask why, I say, "Because I don't like it." I don't want any boy on the field who doesn't want to do what I want him to do. I don't want any boy on the field who doesn't want to please me. I'm not going to ask him to do what's wrong. It's the principle with me. I got sense enough to know that his long hair has nothing to do with his blocking or tackling. But if I can get him to cut his hair or beard off when he doesn't want to cut it, he's giving himself to me. He can give his heart to the Heart Fund, folks, but give me his butt. Then I can make him come to practice on time because he has surrendered to me. He believes in me.

Now, if I'm going to let him tell me what to do, he's going to lose his faith in me. So it's the principle of discipline to me. I don't want any boy on the field who doesn't want to do what I want him to do.

605   I didn't cut a half-dozen boys the whole time I was coaching. We would make pre-season training so tough that they'd quit themselves.

606   If the road is long enough, if the road is rocky enough, the big potato will come to the top and the little potato will go to the bottom.

607   I've been a football coach for 42 years. I've had a chance to see the boy as no mama or papa ever saw. I've seen that boy with his soul stripped naked.

Joe J. Gibbs

Coach: Washington Redskins 1981– . Record: 102-48.

608   The coin toss was probably one of the biggest turning points — *said when Giants, his opponent, won coin toss and elected to kick off with 32 mph wind at team's back.*

609   Awhile back I came to the decision that dealing with people is all football is, so there's no use in getting uptight with things. Can you control these guys? No. They're going to do what they want to do. You just have to set down parameters for them to follow.

610   I'd say handling people is the most important thing you can do as a coach. I've found every time I've gotten into trouble with a player, it's because I wasn't talking to him enough.

611   I was thanking the Lord and I was thinking back to how many hours and how much work had gone into this day — *referring to thoughts after winning '83 Super Bowl.*

612   Don't panic — *said to team, down 10–0 in '88 Super Bowl — they went on to win 42–10 over Denver Broncos.*

613   You start with the ambition of avoiding the two things that kill off the passing game: the sack and the interception. One way to accomplish that is to place your receivers all over the field and have a quarterback with a quick release so well instructed in reading defenses that he always throws into the thinnest part of the coverage. Every pass should have a built-in big play. Why settle for a 12-yard gain if there is a 50-yard gain possible? Multiple receivers give you the flexibility to go for broke on every play.

614   I'm just the hood ornament.

615   Mine was a decision not to grow up—*referring to why he made a career out of coaching.*

616   I never realized how tough it was to tell some of these guys who led you to the Super Bowl that their careers were over.

617   It's a gut-wrenching, throw-up experience every Sunday—*referring to coaching.*

618   Whatever your business is, we all have a drama going on in our lives. We're all unhappy about something. You have sickness, marital problems, a myriad of things going wrong in everybody's life. You have to deal with those things right away. You have to get their full concentration on football. I'd like to be able to communicate even more with my players when things aren't going bad, but it's like just everything else in life. The problems take over and you wind up chasing the problems. I'd say handling people is the most important thing you do as a coach.

619   There are a lot of guys out there working in an office who are extremely competitive.

620   If you go out for dinner, I guarantee you it's an hour and a half out of your day. And if you try to go home and there's a problem, it's longer. This is economical, and it's a real pleasure—*rationale for having dinner catered in coaches' meeting room three nights a week during football season.*

621   After I finished with team sports, it was almost like I was crazed. I had to have something to do. Racquetball filled a void in my life, a personal competitive thing.

622   I think if I was a stockbroker, I'd be playing racquetball and golf all the time. I think a lot of people are that way.

623   My dream as a kid was to play—all the time.

Sidney "Sid" Gillman

Coach: University of Miami (OH) 1944–1947, University of Cincinnati 1949–1954, Los Angeles Rams 1955–1959, Los Angeles/San Diego Chargers 1960–1969 (team moved after '80 season), Houston Oilers 1973–1974. Record: 204-123-9.

624   Some of the players now—I'm not sure whether football is a vocation or an avocation with them. You know what football is to me? It's blood.

625   Game plans, if I had a dollar for every game plan I've drawn up, aw hell, I'd probably still be doing what I'm doing anyway.

626   The first thing you have to know about all game plans is this. They are really not that complicated and they usually are overrated.

627   Basically, there is no magic about a game plan. There is no way you can sit behind a projector for 185 hours or something, and, presto, come up with an idea that's going to make people disappear.

628   The Brinks truck used to stop every 15 minutes at the stadium and haul the money away in a wheelbarrow—*referring to ticket sales to games at the Los Angeles Coliseum in the 1950s.*

629   The most popular pass in pro football today is the option screen pass. It has brought the screen pass back into vogue. The advantage of the play is that a receiver will run a quick pattern, usually about 15 yards, that is timed exactly with the drop of the quarterback. The quarterback has the option of throwing to that receiver downfield for a positive gain. However, if the receiver is covered, the quarterback will have a wall assembled in front of him, and at that point he can still unload a pass to the screen man.

630   The defensive coach has all his people around him and he's playing chess with you. And you're playing chess with him, moving people around.

631   Every team has certain favorite formations. Either the team lines up in those formations or it can move to them from a different formation before the snap. Sometimes motion is simply a device to keep the defense guessing before the snap, or a method to enable the quarterback to make the defense tip its hand about its coverages. But more and more, when a team uses motion, it is very likely a meaningful part of the play.

632   The reason for movement is to create a soft spot someplace. If it doesn't create soft spots for the pass or for the run, then there's no sense to it.

633   What you're looking for is reaction and overreaction on the part of the defense.

634   You build your offense from your basic running game, from what I like to call our "Dirty Dozen." It's as good a name as any for 12 plays we think are the best 12 plays your talent will let us run. We're going to maintain and keep polishing all these basic things because we know them well, and we're going to work like hell on execution. Now we expand our selection to the "Dirty Dozen Plus Four." What's "Plus Four?" It's any special plays we think can be designed to beat the people we're playing. That's the maximum number you might add. It might be only Plus One or Plus Two. The more changes you make, the worse execution you're going to get.

635   We often make the error of thinking we can accomplish something simply by drawing "X's" and "O's." But those "X's" and "O's" don't mean a thing if you don't have the people to carry them out.

636   We haven't been a team of character. We've been a team of characters.

637   How can you possibly make a call like that? You stink, you know that, you stink — *said to an official who walked off 15-yard penalty and replied, "Hey Sid, how do I smell from here?"*

638   I don't want the little play, the average play. I want the big play. Hell, I'm not going to stay up all night trying to figure out how to gain three yards.

639   You put in a lot of hours. There's just no other way.

640   There's one club I worked for that never worked at night. After practice, the day was done. But they started very early in the morning.

641   We're going to drill those plays and we're going to run them so well that on the other side it wouldn't make a hell of a lot of difference if Mohammed, Moses and anybody else was over there.

642   You can't emphasize one and forget the other — *referring to the mental and physical aspects of the game.*

643   They used to say you couldn't tell the players without a program. That's really true now because they're running in and out all the time. Pro football has resolved itself into a special situations game.

644   If you try to go long as a last resort, after other things haven't worked, you usually get in trouble. But if you go long right away, even if you don't hit it, you've put the fear of God into them and probably opened up some other things. The threat of the long pass sets up your passing game.

645   You might run them only once a game, or maybe not at all. But you need the threat of them. The defense needs to know they are there — *referring to trick plays.*

646   Essentially, no matter who you're playing, you have a basic passing game just like your basic running game. You have so many passes to the tight end, so many passes to the strong side end, so many to the weak side end and running backs. It's all patterned.

647   Play action passes are the keys to the big play off the passing game. And big plays win football games.

Harold P. "Bud" Grant

Coach: Winnipeg Blue Bombers (Canadian Football League) 1957–1966, Minnesota Vikings 1967–1983 and 1985. Record: 283-165-8.

648   As coaches, we have no union, no bargaining agent, no protection and no strength to deal from.

649   The thing in the back of your mind, always, is the insecurity.

650   There are coaches who spend 18 hours a day coaching the perfect game, then lose because the ball is oval and they can't control the bounce.

651   It's possible to make up a rule and learn about people by how they react to it. After I told the players about staying off the new sod, I went out on the field and watched. There were players who would come running up to the sodded area, recognize it and go around it. There were players who would run on to it and then stop, you knew they'd forgotten and then remembered what I said after they started across. Those fellows would back up and go around. There were some who could come running out and go across the sodded area without even realizing it. Finally, there were fellows who just roared on across the sodded area, in defiance of what I had said. It's important to learn things like that about people. You learn who the players are who will forget what you tell them, you learn who will remember what you tell them, and you learn who just won't buy what you tell them. The same thing will happen in a game.

652   My "moments" were few and far between, but I was able to make a contribution—*referring to his career with the Minnesota Lakers basketball team, '49–'50.*

653   To understand the kind of game he played last week against the Rams you would have to sit in our film room. You would see a 38-year-old man going full bore from start to finish against one of the best teams in football, and not only against the man assigned to block him. They had a rookie quarterback so they gave him maximum protection by doubling on our defensive ends. They had a 270-pound tackle and a 230-pound back blocking on Marshall. He came charging on every play. I don't know how many times he ran the width of the field chasing a play. We had to substitute for practically everybody on the defensive team at one time or other, but Marshall was still going wide open at the finish.

654   I told him if he was going to play he had to learn how to catch the football. That was all he needed to hear. He just overwhelmed his problem with work . . . he practiced and practiced and practiced until he could catch the ball. It wasn't pretty . . . he'd box it or grab it against his chest but he'd catch it. We were at Detroit once, and Ozzie was running scot-free behind their secondary. He was wide open. I saw the ball in the air, for him, and I died a thousand deaths watching. He spun one way, then the other—he almost fell down but he caught it. Ozzie could make a routine catch look spectacular—*referring to Dave Osborn.*

655   All we can do is learn from it—*said after a loss.*

656   What can happen is that you don't know what's going to happen.

657   You either take the time or you take the consequences—*referring to dealing with the media.*

658   It's up to each man to prepare himself. I can't do that for him.

659   The Super Bowl turns the season into heaven or hell. It's glory or junk for two teams in football.

660   When you make a decision you gather facts and then you weigh them. Everything is a risk if you want to look at it that way, or you can flip it over and say that everything is an opportunity. It's up to you to decide.

661   Tenacity is something that can be maintained so long as you are rewarded for it. If you're having success, even if you're tired, it's easy to remain tenacious.

662   A good coach needs a patient wife, loyal dog and a great quarterback—not necessarily in that order.

663   If I'd known 25 years ago what I know now, I don't know if I'd have gotten into this profession.

664   If you ever field a punt on the two-yard line again, you're out of here—*said to Charlie West, who ran for a 98-yard touchdown after catching the ball.*

665   We wanted to come out of training camp with enthusiasm, not stagger out of it exhausted—*referring to the short time span of his training.*

666   Heat, harassment and three-hour practices—and never a drop of water on the field—*referring to practicing for Bernie Bierman in August at the University of Minnesota.*

667   There are only so many situations you can encounter and you know every one of them has been encountered before. Football and basketball aren't really as structured as baseball—anything can happen. To me, that's a lot of their appeal—*referring to baseball.*

668   Wiseguys and critics or just plain teed-off fans aren't going to listen very seriously to the kind of explanation I've got—*referring to four Super Bowl losses.*

669   Remember, you never have to apologize for losing.

670   If you're going to have a rule, have a reason for it.

671   We all want to be recognized for our accomplishments, but that recognition, unless you guard against it, can carry you further and further away from the attitude that permitted you to become a winner.

672   My feeling about money is, I'd rather work for you for a dollar too little than for a dollar too much. That way, I'm appreciated more.

673   Excellent teams play hard for two to three quarters in a game, while poor teams have to play hard the whole game.

674   When you've got a chance to win the ball game on one play, you go for it. If it goes into overtime, anything can happen.

675   We generate our own heat—*said when team won game in Minnesota in seven-degree weather with 12-mph winds.*

676   There is an advantage to having coached for a long period of time.... I think you become more comfortable with yourself, you come to know yourself, realize your strengths and your limitations. And you realize the emotions you are feeling aren't very different from those someone else is experiencing. You learn that you don't have all the answers, you still look for them, but you admit to yourself that you're never going to have all of them.

677   Just because a team pays the most money doesn't give a guarantee on winning. You placate players with money, but you can't buy them unless they are willing to join the effort.

678   There is no instant success. It is impossible to acquire experience without some losing efforts.

679   I once had a coach who had a theory that man-to-man defense was always the best because he would always know who to blame if something went wrong. We use a zone defense because we feel that we can get to the quarterback or exert enough pressure to make him unload the ball before the zones get too big.

680   I can't afford the luxury of emotion. I don't concern myself with things over which I have no control, like the officiating or the weather or bad breaks that have already happened.

681   It's important that players are treated equally, like your children.

682   Things happen sometimes, and you can't explain them.

683   There has to be more to life than this—*referring to coaching.*

684   There are other coaches who make more money than I do. That's fine. . . . I've always felt that living where you want to live is worth more than dollars.

685   If you tell a man he's good enough and if you tell him that often enough, eventually he'll begin to believe it himself.

686   It's an entertainment form for the people who watch us, and when it's over they go about their business. With the exception of the next morning's paper, there isn't much left of it.

687   It pays well because the entertainment industry pays well, but its importance is not earth shattering.

688   Don't second-guess yourself. In this business, that's the key. If you can say to yourself, "At that time, in the circumstances, it was the right thing to do," then it was the right thing to do. You can't look back.

689   I don't care if they like me, but I want their respect.

690   You go into a game knowing they'll be there. You don't know how many . . . maybe just a few, maybe more. And you don't know what form they will come in. But they'll be there and they are the opportunities to turn a game around. The trick is to watch for them and recognize them and to respond to them.

691   Being a coach . . . I can't say it's unique but it's different than most jobs I know.

A. Forrest Gregg

Coach: Cleveland Browns 1975–1977, Toronto Argonauts (CFL) 1978, Cincinnati Bengals 1980–1983, Green Bay Packers 1984–1987, Southern Methodist 1989– . Record: 84-107-1.

692   I'm demanding but I'm not that demanding—*referring to a comparison between himself and Vince Lombardi.*

693   What we try to do right from the beginning is to leave no doubt in anyone's mind of what his responsibility is and what's expected of him.

694   The defensive end just doesn't try to come straight ahead over you. If he does, you can stay in front of him, and it would take him more than four seconds to get to the passer and the passer throws the ball in less than four seconds. So the end tries tricks. He fakes to the outside, tries to throw you that way, and cuts back to the inside. He may try to circle way out and get the quarterback from behind.

695   There is no quick way to learn; the only teacher is experience.

696   Blitz—we'll send everybody. At one time or another in a ball game, the corner, weak safety, strong safety with one or two linebackers— they'll all be coming. You have to do things that will keep the offense off balance.

697   I don't accept the fact that a team cannot get motivated for every football game. We want to get people up at the same level, Sunday after Sunday after Sunday. You can look at teams that are inconsistent—one week they play as if it's their last and the next week they play as if they have a million to spare.

George S. Halas

Coach: Chicago Bears 1920–1929, 1933–1942, 1946–1955, and 1958–1967 (team was Decatur Staleys in 1920, moved to Chicago in 1921, changed name to "Bears" in 1922). Record: 325-151-31.

698   Wonder of wonders, we paid all our bills and still had seven dollars in the bank—*referring to team's finances at end of 1921 season.*

699   We'd be lucky if we got a paragraph or two in the middle of the sports section—*referring to lack of interest in professional football during the early years of the game.*

700   I doubt if there was a hundred bucks in the whole room—*said about meeting of executives in 1920 to organize a football league.*

701   Staley is offering you a year-round job with the company and a chance to play football and share in the profits of the gate receipts—*said to*

*potential employees of the Staley Manufacturing Co., producers of corn starch,
to lure them into joining the firm and playing football for its team, which helped
promote the product.*

702   We paid a press agent ten dollars to write an account of the
game—*said after Staleys debuted in Wrigley Field.*

703   I figured he would be running for his life, not just for the
money—*referring to the early-day practice of giving George Trafton gate receipts
in a brown paper bag, taking him out of the game with a few minutes left to play
and sending him to the railway station.*

704   I knew then and there that pro football was destined to be a big-
time sport—*said in 1925, when he was in a crowd lined up for tickets to see Red
Grange play for Chicago.*

705   He was to football what Jack Dempsey was to boxing, what Babe
Ruth was to baseball, and what Bobby Jones was to golf—*said of Red
Grange.*

706   Someday, maybe, but not in 1926—*reply when asked about the
possibility of a second professional football team playing in New York City.*

707   More people have seen the Bears play this year than the first 30
years of our existence put together—*said in 1951, when the team's games
began being televised.*

708   Where's a 68-year-old going to find another job, anyway?—*reply
when asked when he was going to retire from coaching.*

709   I knew it was time to quit when I was chewing out the referee and
he walked off the penalty faster than I could keep up with him.

710   Play another year and buy the whole business—*said to a washed-up
player who asked for a loan to buy a half-interest in a business.*

711   What's his address? I'll send him a quart—*said to a player
who knew he was going to be cut, who asked for a loan to buy milk for his
child.*

712   I know you are the greatest football team ever. Now go out and
show the world—*said before 1940 game in which the Bears beat the Redskins,
73–0.*

713   Everything we did, we did right. Everything they did, they did
wrong—*referring to same championship game.*

714   We had to be content with 73–0—*said when fans were shouting for
the Bears to score 80 points.*

715 On our bench a player said, "This is ridiculous, making them look so bad. Take it easy." He was shouted down—*said during same game.*

716 We used so many kickers that one sportswriter said he was waiting for us to bring on Mrs. O'Leary's cow—*said during same game.*

717 Looking at the films, I saw where we could have scored another touchdown—*said during same game.*

718 We were the Monsters of the Midway—*referring to 1940 team.*

719 Good, step on their toes—*said to player who told Halas that opposing team, New York Giants, had put on sneakers after halftime of 1934 game because ground was frozen. Using that tactic, the Giants won.*

720 I'll never get caught like that again—*said to Giants Wellington Mara and coach Steve Owen, who visited Bears locker room the week after the "Sneaker Game" and saw a few dozen sneakers on top of players' lockers.*

721 The only way I can sleep is to think football.

722 When we won, he sent a cable. When we lost, he wrote a letter—*said of Luke Johnson, who co-managed team while Halas was in the Navy during World War II.*

723 He was so young to die, with a future that held so much for him. But Brian made the most of the brief 26 years allotted to him and he will not be forgotten—*said on death of Brian Piccolo of Bears, who had cancer—June 16, 1970.*

724 Well, I sure wouldn't go in there for a dime. But for 60 cents... —*reply when asked why he flipped two quarters into a urinal containing ten cents.*

725 F— the union!

726 I speak no praise for the good loser, the man who says, "Well, I did my best."

727 Football is a game of emotions. For me, that is the heart of its appeal.

728 He had rare ability. He played with dedication. He possessed the old zipperoo—*said of Dick Butkus.*

729 One hundred and sixty-five defenses. Eleven basics, with 15 variations on each one.

730 Nobody who ever gave his best regretted it.

731   It is an advantage to be a member of an organization with great tradition and it is a responsibility to uphold that tradition.

732   Football is only a chapter in players' lives. They should use it to open doors and provide funds for their real life's work.

733   No coach ever changes a winning defense.

734   Bring back those books!—*referring to his team's playbook and said to George Allen after Halas released Allen from his job as assistant coach so Allen could accept head coaching job.*

735   You and Jesus Christ are the only two people I'd ever pay that much money to—*said to Sid Luckman, who got a $6,000 contract in late '39 after graduating from Columbia University.*

736   There have been three great backs in Chicago history—Red Grange, George McAfee and Gale Sayers.

737   Luckman could do it all. Pass, run, kick, defend—and think—*referring to Sid Luckman.*

738   I'd rather be lucky than good.

739   I remember in one game, head down, charging like a bull, Nagurski blasted through two tacklers at a goal line as if they were a pair of old-time saloon doors, through the end zone, and full speed into the brick retaining wall behind it. The sickening thud reverberated throughout the stadium. "That last guy really gave me a good lick," he said to me when he got back to the sideline—*referring to Bronko Nagurski.*

740   He ran so low to the ground that his back was almost parallel to it. And at the moment of contact with a tackler, he dipped his shoulder and brought it up with terrific impact, like an uppercut. It made no difference how much momentum the tackler had or how much he weighed. Bronko's countersmash with his shoulder bounced the tackler off him like rain hitting a tin roof—*referring to Nagurski.*

741   I took my life in my hands just by making a substitution. They all wanted to play offense and defense and for the entire game—*said during the "old days" of football.*

742   Now, boys, this half Trafton will replace Trafton, Hunk Anderson will take over for Hunk Anderson, and Healey, you'll relieve Healey.

743   You are exactly right, and the National Football League is my mistress—*reply to his wife's comment, "You are married to football."*

744   The winter, spring and summer were each a century long—
referring to his loneliness immediately after his wife died.

745   I don't know what I was talking about but I'm sure I was right—
referring to a photo of him arguing with a referee.

746   I do not underrate trivialities.

747   He spoke with such enthusiasm and ingenuity that profanity
became poetry—*said of Larry Brink of the Rams.*

748   He did not apologize for hitting my legs—*said after Halas had got-*
ten away with tripping an opponent running down the sidelines.

749   Of all sports, football most demands teamwork, in every second
of play.

750   You can achieve only that which you will do.

751   Drill—drill—and still more drill are necessary in order to perfect
the fundamentals.

752   The team is the product of every single candidate. It is your duty
to yourself, to your friends and to the team to keep this thought foremost
in mind at all times.

753   These are the things which you should develop within yourself:
aggressiveness, concentration, determination, obedience, reliability and
harmonious cooperation.

754   If somebody slugs you, hit him harder with a legal block. Push the
rules as far as you can but stay within the rules.

755   I put in a phone for George Preston Marshall but somehow our
band stationed itself behind the Redskin bench that day and George
Preston Marshall couldn't make out the messages. When the Giants came
to play, their phone went dead. We promised an investigation. The
telephone company reported the line had been cut at a street junction box.
They said a youth had been seen opening the manhole cover and going
down into the pit. Of course, the Giants claimed the youth was my son,
Mugs. Football does breed suspicion—*said in 1939, when the Bears had to*
let opponents use their "Spy in the Sky" system, which established a phone con-
nection between an analyst/observer high in the stands and the coach on the
sidelines.

756   He's got to push and shove and claw his way past those blockers,
and if somebody gets an unintentional whack in the nose now and then—
well, that's football.

757   They didn't do anything we didn't expect. But we couldn't stop them from doing it—*referring to loss to Green Bay.*

758   Usually we come to Green Bay to bury Caesar, not to praise him—*said at a testimonial dinner for Vince Lombardi.*

759   Football has largely turned from a personal sport into an impersonal business.

760   I see no difference between a spoken agreement and a written agreement.

761   The validity of the contract was the real issue. Now I want to drop this suit and give Allen his full release. He can go to Los Angeles and he goes with my blessing—*said after victory in breach of contract case against George Allen, who wanted "out" from contract as assistant coach with Halas to become head coach of the Rams.*

762   When the day ends and I say "Good night," few players think of anything except going to bed—*referring to his policy of working players hard during training.*

763   Being fit is fun and adds years to a life.

Thomas J. "Tom" Hamilton

Coach: Navy 1934–1936 and 1946–1947, University of Pittsburgh 1951 and 1954. Record: 28-32-1.

764   A tie is like kissing your sister.

Jim Hanifan

Coach: St. Louis Cardinals 1980–1985, Atlanta Falcons 1989. Record: 39-54-1.

765   What he can't do is get rid of the players. So he's got to make a change and it's the coaches who go. It's always been that way and it's always going to be that way.

Richard E. "Dick" Hanley

Coach: Haskell Institute 1922–1926, Northwestern 1927–1934, Chicago Rockets 1946. Record: 92-41-11.

766   Gentlemen—and I call you this because you have been playing such polite football—people play this game for diverse reasons. Some wish to be popular at tea parties. Some hope for a better job someday. Some wish to prove they are men. Why you play I cannot say, but today this team is immortal. At halftime you became the first football team in Northwestern history to be booed off the field by your classmates, your schoolmates, your brothers. I ask you to go back on that field and show these people that you are men, not quitters—*said when team was losing 14–7 at halftime. It won 32–14.*

Richard C. "Dick" Harlow

Coach: Penn State 1915–1917, Colgate 1922–1925, Western Maryland 1926–1934, Harvard 1935–1942 and 1945–1947. Record: 150-68-17.

767   Sound fundamentals and common sense are what make winning football teams.

768   Do it my way, dear boy.

W. Woodward "Woody" Hayes

Coach: Denison 1946–1948, Miami (OH) 1949–1950, Ohio State 1951–1978. Record: 238-72-10.

769   The eventual winner, we called him. We talked about what kind of football player he'd have made. We even talked about what position he'd have played. We decided on defensive tackle. He could have used those strong, rail-splitter's arms to shed blockers—*referring to Abraham Lincoln.*

770   Me, I can't be nice and win. It's not my way.

771   It appears you didn't get the game plan down pat during the week, so you're going to get it now—*said during a break at halftime, when, instead of resting his men, Hayes took them out to a practice field for a ten-minute scrimmage.*

772   These kids fill Ohio Stadium six times a year, 87,000 and more each Saturday. When you consider the total take, we're not investing much in the product, are we?—*referring to cost of recruiting.*

773   There's no place for cheap shots in football.

774 I don't agree with those 28 "no" votes but I respect the integrity of the men who cast them, if not their intelligence—*referring to the 28 faculty members who voted down an invitation for Ohio State to play in the '62 Rose Bowl, objecting to an overemphasis on sports at the school.*

775 Did I turn in the team that cheated in the league? You're damn right I did. And I'll do it again—*said after reporting Michigan State to the NCAA for recruiting violations.*

776 I like to see our people leave here and go out and help make the world a better place for the generations to come. Some folks say that's corny and a lot of bunk, but it's true. The football will take you only so far. Sometime later on you have to quit that and go on to something else. You can't play forever.

777 Ring the doorbells—*referring to recruiting.*

778 Paralyze their resistance with your persistence.

779 If we bring a young man to our university and don't make sure he gets an education, we're cheating him.

780 I had a Cadillac offered to me one year. You know how that works. They give you a Cadillac one year and the next year they give you the gas to get out of town.

781 We got beaten by a better team. One point better—*said after 18–17 loss to USC in the Rose Bowl.*

782 Anyone who will tear down sports will tear down America.

783 Undoubtedly, too many boys are being tendered scholarships who just aren't students enough to know or even care about what the primary purpose of college is all about—which is to get a meaningful education.

784 One of the most important elements in a football player's ability is strength, but even though pure weight lifters are the strongest guys around they'd be lousy football players. Do you know why? Because as big and powerful as they are, they couldn't produce. They're too egocentric. They could never subject themselves to a team principle. They couldn't sacrifice. They like to stand in front of mirrors and admire their muscles, but they couldn't take getting hit.

785 Now the greatest player I ever had playing for me was Hop Cassidy and Hop Cassidy was also about the smallest who ever played for me.

786 Man has to dominate. There's just no other way—*referring to male-female relationships.*

787   Now go back to the Battle of Salamis, where the Greeks beat the tail off the Persians. Now doesn't that take in so many of the things used in football: fear, determination, backs to the wall, home field advantage—all those things you see in a football game, and that Battle of Salamis wasn't for the national championship; it was for the world championship.

788   I didn't say a single word. I hummed and hung up—*said when he called his wife and hummed, "California, Here I Come," immediately after being told not to say a word about his team's Rose Bowl selection until an official announcement.*

789   We all should make a more thorough study of history and we'd be a lot better equipped to handle today and tomorrow.

790   Did you ever hear a better locker room speech?—*referring to Winston Churchill's World War II address to Parliament, which included the words, "We shall fight them on the beaches...."*

791   I see my job as part of American civilization and a damn important part.

792   There is a segment of society which is not only against football but against anything that's well organized.

793   We use a bit of psychology at Ohio State when it appears that some bad feelings are developing between one of our kids and one of the other team. We send in word to our player to pick up his man after the next block or tackle. It's hard to play dirty against a man who picks you up.

794   I don't think it's possible to be too intent on winning. If we played for any other reason, we would be totally dishonest. This country is built on winning and on that alone. Winning is still the most honorable thing a man can do.

795   Winning is the epitome of group effort.

796   I used to be dead against athletic dormitories. I didn't think athletes should be segregated—that they should be exposed instead to the full cross-section of all students. But now I wonder if the athletic dorm isn't the right answer. It gives a coach a better shot at discipline, unity of purpose and at least a small refuge against what goes on in the free-style life the colleges have come to.

797   A year or so ago it was discovered that a male student here had had a girl living with him for several weeks in his dormitory room. University officials were upset. In fact, they were very upset. And do you know why? Because she'd been living there without paying room rent.

798   I didn't come here for the security. I came here for the opportunity—*said when he joined Ohio State.*

799   I've never seen a football player who isn't a better football player than he thinks he is. And as a coach it's my job to make a kid realize his potential.

800   I build my kids up—even though I do get a little rough on them out there on the practice field when they're not performing as well as I think they're capable of. And when I explode I'm telling this: "The only reason I'm mad is because I know you can do better. You can do more." So the implication is always positive, no matter how I deliver it.

801   You see, the thing is, I'm not interested in exposing people and taking away their jobs. I just want to bring people in compliance with the rules—*referring to why he didn't talk when he learned other coaches had broken rules.*

802   You see, the older you get, the more you see that rules are just the only thing holding up this society.

803   A horse can't go to the starting gate chewing on his oats—*referring to the benefits of "butterflies in the stomach" before the start of the game.*

804   Winning takes care of everything.

805   You can't pay back, but you can pay forward.

806   I like to feel that I can get the best out of a football player. Maybe you'd call me a human engineer. I believe I can recognize talent, then use it.

807   You know it really takes the edge off a football player when there's a warm little ass next to him in bed. I know it's true because I've done some research on it.

808   No one will outwork me.

809   I try to get six or seven hours of sleep a night and I try not to miss any meals. But just about all the time that's left goes to football.

810   You see, I try to talk my coaches out of things and if I can't, then I know they're really sure of themselves.

811   It's no good for the mother to be away from the home.

812   All players simply don't learn at the same rate of speed or with the same degree of mastery. If we see a player making a mistake we just don't get him out of there and run the play with somebody else just because the first kid doesn't learn very fast. That would be an indictment of our coaches. We just think we've got to spend extra time on the player.

813   If they can get it inside their helmets, they can wear it. When they can no longer do that, we'll have to make new decisions—*said about Afro haircuts.*

814   Every man should be up and thinking by seven o'clock in the morning.

815   We were getting the hell knocked out of us in the North Atlantic (during World War II) because all our naval training had been done down in the sunny Caribbean. We couldn't fight in cold weather. Then the Navy got a new chief of staff and he switched all the maneuvers to the North Atlantic. We got tougher and started winning. So from now on, this football team is practicing in the North Atlantic, no matter how cold it gets. No Caribbean for us—*said in response to request to hold practice indoors because of cold weather.*

816   Sports and religion have made America what it is today.

817   Statistics always remind me of the fellow who drowned in the river whose average depth was only three feet.

818   It's never an upset if the so-called underdog has all along considered itself the better team.

819   It was an even game played on an uneven field—*said of a tie game played at the University of Michigan, with fans rooting for the home team.*

820   Some people change and some people change too late, and then you have a problem. Like the one we had in Newcomerstown (Ohio) when they had to give up driver's ed in the high school because the horse died.

821   How would you like it if they did this to you all the time?—*said while punching a member of a TV crew who pushed a camera in his face.*

822   I can see why a good photographer would be almost as eager to get good pictures as a coach is to win a football game, and I am sorry that our intentions came into conflict; for photographic display is certainly an integral part of our game of football—*part of letter of apology for knocking down a photographer in '73.*

823   I try not to be petty, but I am a petty person. And I have a terrible temper.

824   You see, this has been my whole life. I mean, all of it. I love it. I love the challenge. I love the fact that I'm busy. I love the fact that I'm never bored with it.

825 Pride is a great thing to have. No real football player should be without it.

826 All truly great athletes have an inner confidence.

827 We control by attitudes, not by rules.

828 Every time I've talked to a writer I've regretted it because you fellows end up twisting everything.

829 To me there's nothing worse than being laughed at.

830 Civilization without heroes isn't going to be a civilization much longer.

831 The problem comes from people believing they have too many rights, and the word "rights" to them means acting like an idiot—*said after Wisconsin fans threw objects on field while their team was losing to Ohio State.*

832 We don't have many heroes nowadays and sometimes if we do they're the wrong kind.

833 The classroom professor gives a final examination once each semester, right? In essence, he has been preparing his class for that final exam, right? Well, you can also claim that the way that class is going to perform in that examination is a reflection of his success in preparing those kids for it. I don't care whether it's history, economics or Russian literature. If a number of his students do poorly, by gosh, I say that professor has done poorly. Now take the football coach. What he's doing is giving a final examination not just once a semester but every week for at least ten weeks. His expertise as a teacher is on the line every Saturday.

834 What was I supposed to do, lie to them or tell them what I really believed?—*referring to controversy caused after '54 Rose Bowl when he said six Big Ten teams were better than his opponent, the University of Southern California.*

835 We provide wonderful publicity for the university.

836 If you study the history of the world, as I have, you'll find our revolution was the only really successful one, because it never got out of the hands of the moderates. You have to have moderate people to keep things on the right track.

William W. "Pudge" Heffelfinger

Coach: University of California 1893, Lehigh 1894, University of Minnesota 1895.
Record: 18-12-1.

837   For head guards we just let our hair grow and pulled it through a turtleneck sweater.

838   It was not unusual for a man to play for eight or so years for the same school. No one thought anything of it. Everyone was doing it— *referring to college football in the 1880s and '90s.*

839   The secret to line play is your stance. Both on attack and defense you have to stand more or less erect, knees bent in a slight crouch, boldly leaning forward from the hips, legs spread about three feet apart, left foot advanced when playing left guard.

840   A man is no good on his knees.

841   It's method, not muscle, that will give you the jump on linemen.

842   By watching the ball closely, you can detect the slightest flexing of the opposing center's hands—the tipoff that he's going to snap it—and in this way time your charge with the ball.

843   I never kept my head down. I wanted to see what was coming and be up on my feet where I could deliver.

844   My old coach, Walter Camp, used to tell us on defense, "Let them have two yards." To which I'd reply, "No sir, not two inches."

845   A standing line helps screen the ball carrier.

846   Take no chances. Kick on first down. A fumble here may cost you the game—*referring to gaining possession inside your ten-yard line.*

847   I never made a blind charge. I drove in toward the pressure point and mussed things up before the interference could form. If you hit 'em first you catch 'em off balance.

848   Sheer speed is not worth much unless you apply it in bursts. Stop-go runners are the fellows who fake the tackler into bow knots.

849   He reminded me of a wise old mule in a pasture with a bunch of horses. The mule may look dumb, but he sees everything out of the corner of his eye—*said of Bronko Nagurski.*

850   A man's body must go where his head goes.

851   A game that can keep you young and vibrant and all steamed up is a precious thing.

John W. Heisman

Coach: Oberlin 1892 and 1894, Akron 1893, Auburn 1895–1899, Clemson 1900–1903, Georgia Tech 1904–1919, University of Pennsylvania 1920–1922, Washington and Jefferson 1923, Rice 1924–1927. Record: 185-70-17.

852   I had seen the first forward pass in football. It was illegal, of course—*referring to a game in 1895.*

853   Once a game started, a player could not leave unless he actually was hurt, or at least, pleaded injury. Accordingly, whenever the captain wanted to put a fresh player into action, he whispered, "Get your arm hurt, or something." In one game, my captain whispered to me, "Get your neck broke, Heisman"—*referring to his playing days in the late 1880s and early '90s.*

854   We had no helmets or pads of any kind; in fact, one who wore homemade pads was regarded as a sissy.

855   Time was when we fooled the enemy by having the quarterback pass a tan helmet to one of his halfbacks and the ball to another.

856   When in doubt, punt.

857   I have played football more than 40 years and more than three-quarters of that long time I have devoted to coaching. I started coaching hopeful of making it clear to my men that offense means charging and blocking, and that defense means charging and fighting. And not once during those years of coaching have I had to alter that prescription by a single word.

858   Good tackling is nothing but scientific tripping. You stop your man not by meeting his force with yours but by taking his legs out from beneath him.

859   I've known men and women who were as bitterly opposed to football as they were to prizefighting and for a very similar reason—its alleged brutality. And then they saw a game.

860   Thrust your projections into their cavities.

861   At times he must be severe, arbitrary, little short of a tzar—*referring to the role of a coach.*

862   ...leave 'em for dead!

863   What is it? A prolate spheroid, an elongated sphere, one in which the outer leathern casing is drawn tightly over a somewhat smaller rubber tubing. Better to have died as a small boy than to fumble this football.

864   The true football fan pays no attention to time, mileage and so on when there is a big game to see.

865   A dangerous goal kicker is a marked man.

866   I've seen moral courage in football as often as physical. I've seen football make men out of condemned material.

Elmer C. "Gus" Henderson

Coach: Southern California 1919–1924, Tulsa 1925–1935, Los Angeles Bulldogs 1937, Detroit Lions 1939, Occidental 1940–1942. Record: 140-47-7.

867   Good coaching, like the effect of cigarettes, always tells in the long run.

Howard "Red" Hickey

Coach: San Francisco 49ers 1959–1963. Record: 27-27-1.

868   Anyone can catch a ball in practice when he knows he won't be hit.

Herman Hickman

Coach: Yale University 1948–1951. Record: 16-18-2.

869   You may not have the best football coach in the country, but you sure got the biggest—*said when he began coaching Yale—and weighed 320 pounds.*

870   The values are a little different up here. For instance, can you imagine 80,000 coming out to see two teams play that have won only four games between them? They came to see Yale play Harvard last fall. Tradition, son. We may not have much, but we got a lot of tradition. You can't eat it and you can't drink it, but it's there.

871   You know, there's just a lot of people that feel I know more about food than I do about football.

872   Those were the days when our hearts were young and gay. How long ago was that? Well, I would say about 50 pounds ago.

873   Yale is a mighty good school, high standards, quality students, finest crop of ivy you ever saw and more scholarships than anybody, for people who don't play football. Now they don't hold it against you at Yale if you play football. But it don't do you any good.

874   We went into the last periods leading both Harvard and Princeton, but I gathered the boys around me and said, "Fellows, how about losing this one for old Herman?" Bless 'em, they obliged.

875   His record down at the hospital looks like a research project—*said of a player who went to the infirmary 15 times with injuries.*

876   I wanna see blood.

877   I'll eat anything that can't eat me.

878   It doesn't give the alumni anything to look forward to next season—*said of a perfect year with no losses.*

879   My motto is: Keep 'em hungry! I like 'em sullen, but not mutinous!—*said of alumni.*

880   I'll tell you, son. Sit down here and repeat after me: "Our Father, who art in heaven . . ."—*reply to player asking, "What can we do now, coach?" after Yale's defensive strategy resulted in two quick Princeton touchdowns.*

881   In modern football you can't win with iron men anymore. I have three special teams—one for offense, one for defense and one to hit the books.

882   I just wish that some of them had my thyroid—*said after looking at the small size of Yale football players.*

883   There will be only one excuse for lateness and that's death. I mean personal deaths, not professional ones.

884   You can't afford me and I ain't worth it—*said to discourage organizations from booking him for speaking engagements.*

885   I just memorize things for fun. I guess I know more useless information than anyone who lives. I love history and poetry.

886   Ye call me chief and ye do well to call me chief. If ye are men, follow me. Strike down your guard, gain the mountain passes and there do bloody work as did your sires at old Thermopylae. Is Sparta dead? Is the old Grecian spirit frozen in your veins that you do crouch and cower like a belabored hound beneath his master's lash? Oh, comrades, warriors, Thracians! If we must fight, let us fight for ourselves. If we must slaughter, let us slaughter our oppressors. If we must die, let it be under the clear sky, by the bright waters, in noble, honorable battle. Whaddya say, let's go chew up those Harvards—*said as pep talk before a game against Harvard. It was Spartacus' oratory to the gladiators.*

887   It always has been and always will be an exhibition—*said of professional wrestling.*

888   I have seen more violent reactions from fans at a wrestling match than I ever saw or heard during a football game.

889   I still don't think you can get a better night's entertainment than you will by seeing your favorite hero tangle with a villain. This plot has been the longest run in show business so it must have something.

890   A mere scientific exhibition of clean wrestling still won't draw at the gate. There must be a hero and a villain.

891   As entertainment it is usually better than a lot of movies and it should not have a bad influence on any member of the family because virtue is always supreme.

892   I want to digress just one moment here and say that I've been mixed up in many kinds of enterprises since my wrestling days and have met many kinds of people, but none can compare with the wrestlers for generosity, friendliness and real straight shooting.

893   All the wrestlers had code names ... I was Cannonball.

894   I was presented as the clean-cut college boy type and because of my football background, the flying tackle was my key hold.

895   Wild Bill refused to shake hands with me in the center of the ring before the match. The crowd booed. He complained about the oil on my ears and hair. The crowd booed. He had an argument with the referee about what constituted a fall in the state of New York and threatened to leave the ring. The crowd hated him already—*said of his opponent in his wrestling debut.*

896   *Question:* What becomes of old broken-down wrestlers? *Answer:* They are still wrestling.

897   Walk four blocks to an appointed rendezvous, where two of the boys are waiting in an automobile. Drive a couple more blocks and pick up your opponent. He was disqualified for choking you just an hour ago— *referring to pro wrestlers traveling from city to city in the 1930s.*

898   When my friend, Peahead Walker, was coaching at Wake Forest, a player gets stretched out cold. Peahead and the doctor run out on the field. "Drag him off," says Peahead, "a dead man can't play football." "He ain't even breathing," says the doctor. "You're the doctor, ain't ya?" roars Peahead. "Make him breathe."

899   You know, down south we had a baseball coach who lost 38 games in a row. Finally the college president called him on the carpet and asked for an explanation. The coach banged on the president's desk and demanded, "What do you expect a fellow to do? Win them all?"

900   Back in 1941 they were holding maneuvers down in Tennessee. The Red Army and Blue Army were fighting for Hill 101. And on top of Hill 101 was Uncle Joe's cabin. He was sitting in his cabin, squirting tobacco juice in the fire, as the two armies started shelling the hill. The shells came closer and closer. Finally one landed right under the window. Uncle Joe had stood it as long as he could. He rushed out the door, threw up his hands and cried, "I don't give a damn what Robert E. Lee said, I surrender."

901   Dopey's granddaddy was a diehard Confederate colonel. When he heard that Dopey was going to West Point, the old man fought the move tooth and nail. Finally, the colonel gave in, saying, "All right, Joel, go up there with those Yankees, if you must. But remember this: Learn everything you can about their ammunition. Learn everything about their guns. Learn everything about their tactics—because we ain't lost this war yet!"

902   Can't tell too many of my kinfolk stories anymore. Got ivy on my walls now.

903   The players you don't get seem to be the ones you remember best—*said of recruiting.*

904   Beast barracks could be politely described, perhaps, as a basic training period or indoctrination course. I have heard it referred to by plebes in cruder terms—*said while Hickman was an assistant coach at West Point.*

905   Thirty years ago you were considered yellow if you tackled above the knees.

906   Why not mix fun with football whenever you can.

Michael J. "Mike" Holovak

Coach: Boston College 1951–1959, New England Patriots 1961–1968, New York Jets 1976. Record: 103-76-12.

907   If I knew what we were doing wrong, I'd have done something about it.

908   Every team has thrown against us, but this team ran too.

Louis L. "Lou" Holtz

Coach: William & Mary 1969–1971, North Carolina State 1972–1975, New York Jets 1976, University of Arkansas 1977, University of Minnesota 1984–1985, Notre Dame 1986– . Record: 156-86-5.

909   They call me "The Great Motivator." I'll tell you how to motivate. It's simple. You eliminate those who aren't motivated.

910   Red-shirting has brought about a greater change in college football than anything I've seen in my entire coaching career. That extra year gives them a tremendous advantage.

911   If we're behind, we'll switch to Plan B. But you have to remember that if Plan B was any good, we would have used it in the first place.

912   The only thing universal about alumni is that they end every season with "but." Like, "We had a good season, but..."

913   You never get ahead of anyone as long as you try to get even with him.

914   It makes a tougher target for the fans to hit—*reply when asked why he crouched down on the sidelines.*

915   In the successful organization, no detail is too small to receive close attention.

916   If there is one absolute in our society, I think it's that abuse leads to restrictions. Most rules and laws in our society derive from the fact that too many people did not have the self-discipline to refrain from taking advantage of the liberties this country offers.

917   If there were any cuss words or variations of them I'd never heard him use before, he sure trotted them out now. Man, what a job he did on me. He wound up telling me I was fired right then and there. Then he stormed off before I could say a word in my own defense, not that he'd have accepted any. I was lower than a whale's belly and I asked a couple of the other coaches whether I should just take a plane back to Columbus or whether I'd be allowed to go back on the team plane. They just laughed. They said unless Woody put it in writing I should forget it. So I just showed up at practice that day with my knees knocking, waiting for Woody to set eyes on me. He acted as though nothing had happened—*said about incident while working as assistant coach for Woody Hayes at Ohio State.*

918   You praise loudly and criticize softly.

919   Your athletes are going to respond one way or the other, depending on whether you coach them positively or not. There are no average athletes. There are only athletes who think they are average. Give your athletes something they can do physically and coach the living hell out of them positively.

920   Don't be a spectator, don't let life pass you by.

921   Sit up or get out.

922   I never wanted to be too rich, because I'd be afraid of losing it, or too poor. Notre Dame has made both objectives possible.

923   The Notre Dame coach is treated with great respect—initially.

924   I think it's just a signal that one of the prerequisites to be a coach at Notre Dame is that you can't cry—*referring to eye duct problems.*

925   Don't tell me how rocky the sea is. Just bring the gol durned ship in.

926   You can't have everybody wanting to get the damned ball on a pass. And you can't have individualism on your team.

927   Your social life must be nonexistent during the season—*said to his players.*

928   Self-discipline is the greatest asset an individual can possess.

929   You cannot win without good athletes, but you can lose with them. This is where coaching can make the difference.

930   In recruiting, we try to sell 40 years, not just four.

931   I don't mind starting the season with unknowns. I just don't like finishing a season with a bunch of them.

932   Don't ever ask a player to do something he doesn't have the ability to do, because he'll question your ability as a coach, not his as an athlete.

933   I have never thought of leaving Arkansas since I got here. Suicide, yes. Leaving, no.

934   Coaching is nothing more than eliminating mistakes before you get fired.

935   According to the Bible, Joseph died leaning on his staff, and I think the same will be said of me.

936   If you can't hug them, pat them and brag about them, you don't want them on your team.

937   If they laugh, they're with you.

938   I try not to ask people things. I tell them. See, I'm the coach.

939   When you win, you have as many problems as when you lose. They are just different problems.

940   Not everybody can be first team, but you can always put the team first.

941   We have been married to each other for 56 years, 28 apiece — *referring to his wife.*

942   Your value to the team is inversely proportionate to your distance from the ball.

943   The only things that are going to change you from where you are today to where you are going to be five years from now are the people you meet and the books you read.

944   We all have more talent than we will probably ever use.

945   I have a lifetime contract. That means I can't be fired during the third quarter if we're ahead and moving the ball.

946   If you don't make a total commitment to whatever you're doing, then you start looking to bail out the first time the boat starts leaking. It's tough enough getting that boat to shore with everybody rowing, let alone when a guy stands up and starts putting his life jacket on.

947   When all is said and done, more is said than done.

948   You're never as good as everyone tells you when you win, and you're never as bad as they say when you lose.

949   Keep a low profile. If you're any good, people will talk about you.

950   Golf is probably the most difficult game in this world to play.

951   Don't count the days, make the days count.

952   Officials are the only factor I know of in a game you can't neutralize.

953   I haven't had a chance to read it, but if it's unfavorable then we have to assume it's true—*referring to a front-page article about him in the* Wall Street Journal.

954   I couldn't convince him they weren't any different from winters in Arkansas—unless you went outside—*referring to his inability to take assistant Bob Shaw with him when he moved from Arkansas to Minnesota.*

955   We will get the heart and soul of our football team from the state of Minnesota. However, we'll have to go elsewhere for the arms and legs.

956   I've always been in favor of having a two-team—or maximum four-team—playoff at the completion of the Bowls.

957   The man who complains about the way the ball bounces is likely the one who dropped it.

958   I'm always real leery of schools that have letter abbreviations. They always seem to be real good.

959   The only way people are going to stop us from getting the ball to Brown is if they intercept the snap from center—*referring to flanker Tim Brown.*

960   What a great day for work. I tell you, people come to South Bend for vacation—*said during a windy, rainy day.*

961   I don't think you're fat. But I do think for your weight, you should be nine, three.

962   Playing at home is only an advantage if you win. If you lose, you're better off playing on the road because you have a better chance of getting out of the stadium alive.

963   The graveyards are full of indispensable people.

964   There's only one bright side of losing—the phone doesn't ring as much the following week.

965   We were the only school in America that lost more football games than students—*referring to his first year at Notre Dame, when the school lost six students.*

966   I wasn't a good enough athlete to attend Notre Dame for football and I certainly wasn't smart enough to get in academically. But isn't it ironic that I'm smart enough to coach at Notre Dame? I guess the standards for being a coach are lower than those to be a student.

967   You win a couple and they want to put you in the hall of fame. You lose two and they think you're deemphasizing football.

968   Discipline is what you do for someone, not to someone. Then they have the option of getting better or bitter.

969   I start off in the morning with my heart sounding like this: boom and boom and boom and boom. By the time I get to practice, it's like this: boomaboomaboomaboom, boom.

970   If I was murdered as soon as practice was over, there would be so many suspects among the players that they wouldn't even try to investigate.

971   If they kidnapped me and said I was being held captive in my office, my wife would believe them. And she'd probably pay the ransom just to see me . . . I should hope she'd pay it . . . I think she'd pay it if it wasn't too high.

972   First we will be best, then we will be first.

973   We aren't where we want to be, we aren't where we ought to be, but, thank goodness, we aren't where we used to be—*referring to Notre Dame's team.*

974   You can't be a miracle worker. You do the best you can and you go from there.

975   This is the biggest game today. There will be a bigger one tomorrow.

976   You know whether it's in business, politics, education or athletics, there has to be respect and loyalty for the leader. Success or failure depends on it. There are three questions from the leader that must be answered affirmatively by individual group members if the group needs assurance that it can reach its desired goal. Can I trust you? Are you committed? Do you respect or care about me?

977   Successful people never make excuses.

978   One day you are drinking the wine and the next day you are picking the grapes.

Jim Lee Howell

Coach: New York Giants 1954–1960. Record: 54–29–4.

979   All I did was pump up footballs—*referring to his job as coach of New York Giants, when Tom Landry and Vince Lombardi were his assistants.*

980   He would just sit there and burn inside—*referring to Tom Landry, his assistant coach at the Giants.*

981   You've got to punish your man to make him respect you.

982   It was healthy as far as I was concerned, an incentive for each of them to do as well as they could—*referring to the rivalry between assistant coaches Landry and Lombardi.*

983   It takes two to make a fight. I tried to make the officials see my side of it, but they didn't—*said when he thought player was kicked while down.*

984   Nobody was ever more reliable on third and short. That man knew it would be tough. He knew they were waiting for him. He knew it was going to hurt. But he just threw his body in the hole and he fought for the yardage. And he never complained about injuries. He was one tough bastard—*referring to Alex Webster.*

William B. "Bill" Ingram

Coach: William and Mary 1922, University of Indiana 1923–1925, Navy 1926–1930, University of California 1931–1934. Record: 75-42-9.

985   Water? Water? What you need is fire, not water—*reply when his men asked for water during practice.*

Bill Johnson

Coach: Cincinnati Bengals 1976–1978. Record: 18-15.

986   You know, we've had players talk over the years about being in a business or sport that dehumanizes them and all sorts of bunk like that. No man can be dehumanized unless he lets it happen to him.

987   I like to think that I'm close to them, but by the very nature of my job there's a natural separation.

988   Principle will win tough games. There's so much adversity in this business that you have to have principles.

989   It's a long, tough grind. I really don't believe the average fan comes close to understanding what it takes out of a player to stick it out.

990   I believe people of strong convictions are winners, and I like that.

991   I had a coach not long ago tell me he took every one of our game films and copied down our entire offense just because he liked the way we did it. And so what?

992   Lots of people have ability, but often something sidetracks them and takes away some of that talent.

993   Perhaps the most difficult adjustment a player coming out of college has to make is the realization that everyone in the pros is talented. Everyone has ability. Everyone is an exceptional player.

994   Years ago there were lots of long runs, but not any longer. The game is too fast. The defenses are too quick, and they just don't let you get loose for the long ones.

995   It's a game of skill, but it's a game of emotion, a game of mental discipline and preparedness. All things being even, the team with the mental edge will win.

996   In a lot of ways, football hasn't changed a bit since I pulled on my first uniform back in the sixth grade in Tyler, Texas. It still requires toughness and dedication and all that. And the teams that have the most discipline, and block and tackle best, still win. But the game has become much more sophisticated, much more complex, and in many ways the pressures on the people in the game have become intensified. I look at some rookies and I know they're scared. They have every right to be. It can be a scary experience. It's a different world, one of almost total isolation. I've never known a player to last very long in the National Football League without being a real man.

997   Pro football is a sport, sure, but it's a business. And it's a tough business. You've been on campus where the atmosphere is pretty much a fun thing, and you're with your own age group. Suddenly you're tossed into a whole new set of circumstances. You have a total environment change. You're in with older men, some of them approaching 40 years old. They're professionals, and have been for a long time. They're pretty proficient at what they do. And, to be truthful, they're a pretty protective group. It's a tough thing to say, maybe, but it's a dog-eat-dog business. I never thought of it as a culture shock, but I guess in reality that's what it is. Pro football is a rigorous, mental routine. It's a game for really tough people. You're separated from your family, you're in a full-time profession, and the mental discipline required is staggering.

Howard H. Jones

Coach: Syracuse 1908, Yale 1909 and 1913, Ohio State 1910, University of Iowa 1916–1923, Duke 1924, Southern California 1925–1940. Record: 194-64-21.

998   Lick a man and hold your position. You have a spot about a yard or two on either side of you to see that nobody gets through. No matter who winds up with the ball, they don't go anywhere if you guard your own small territory and don't get faked out trying to find where the ball is at.

999   I prohibit the boys from hanging around poolrooms because the air in such places is usually bad and his associates are not always of the best.

1000   The objections I have against dancing are: first, it breaks in upon sleeping and eating; second, it is a different form of exercise than the boy is used to and is tiring; third, there is the danger of getting heated up and then cooling off too quickly; fourth, a midnight lunch is usually partaken of, mostly because of obligations to the girl; fifth, the boy usually does not feel like getting up for breakfast.

1001   I like to hear a squad singing popular songs after a hard practice and while dressing.

1002   Nothing is more harmful to the morale of the squad while scrimmaging than the agonizing cry of an injured man. A good rule to follow is to keep still until one is sure he's hurt, and then not yell the information from the housetops, but to report quietly to the physician in charge.

1003   Those who say players spend too much time on football when they should be studying should remember that a student who lets the game come between himself and an education wouldn't study anyway.

Thomas Albert Dwight "Tad" Jones

Coach: Syracuse University 1909–1910, Yale University 1916 and 1920–1927. Record: 66-24-6.

1004   You are about to play football for Yale against Harvard. Never in your lives will you do anything so important.

1005 No matter what happens, the important thing is that you come off the field knowing you have made a total commitment.

Ralph "Shug" Jordan

Coach: Auburn 1951–1975. Record: 176-83-6.

1006 And let me promise you that if I was dying, I'd sure as hell find a better way to spend my last days than answering a bunch of questions from you people—*response to reporter who said Jordan looked unhealthy and asked if he was dying.*

1007 Remember, Goliath was a 40-point favorite over Little David but Little David knocked him on his can.

Andrew "Andy" Kerr

Coach: Stanford University 1922–1923, Washington and Jefferson 1926–1928, Colgate 1929–1946, Lebanon Valley 1947–1949. Record: 152-80-15.

1008 We were undefeated, untied, unscored on and uninvited—*referring to fact that Colgate was not asked to '32 Rose Bowl.*

1009 At the center of my philosophy of life has been the idea of service; the desire to help my fellow men. . . . I believe in God, the creator and ruler of the universe. I hold that a man's religious faith is the greatest single force in his life for good.

1010 These fellows are too big and experienced for the average college team, but I think a squad with a lot of manpower, like Southern California, Michigan or Notre Dame, would give them all the competition they want—*said in 1933, when comparing his college team to the pros.*

Charles R. "Chuck" Knox

Coach: Los Angeles Rams 1973–1977, Buffalo Bills 1978–1982, Seattle Seahawks 1983– . Record: 162-109-1.

1011 Nobody has it tougher than a high school coach.

1012   My biggest complaint about high school coaching had nothing to do with buses and players, though. It had to do with there not being enough time to coach. You had to take roll in classes, monitor study hall and fill out truancy reports.

1013   Whatever nickel they make, it isn't enough—*said of high school coaches.*

1014   The job of a high school football coach is not to make his own fortune but to build others' futures.

1015   He who lives in hope, dies in crap.

1016   The last guy with the chalk wins.

1017   Everything must be planned; nothing good happens by accident.

1018   Players, not coaching, wins. But poor coaches lose.

1019   Proper preparation prevents piss-poor performance.

1020   It's not how far you've come, but what kind of trail you've left.

1021   Sure I deal in clichés and everybody mostly makes fun of them. But they remember them.

1022   My little sayings, any little sayings, are effective only through spaced repetition.

1023   Conservative coaches have one thing in common: they are unemployed.

1024   They say the breaks all even up in the long run. But how many of us last that long?

1025   They know the devil they've got, but they forget to think about the devil they're going to bring in next—*referring to the frequent firing of football coaches.*

1026   This is your new quarterback. He gets hurt, you're fired—*how he introduced Joe Namath to the Jets when he was the team's assistant coach.*

1027   Pick a guy and let it fly—*passing advice to Joe Namath.*

1028   A head coach must create a climate in which ideas can be freely offered without any danger of a sarcastic reply, without any danger of ridicule.

1029   I don't want a one-way street on my staff.

1030   Too much looking back and you're going back.

1031   A head coach should know and respect his assistant coaches like he does his heartbeat.

1032   You have 285-pound guards jumping down your throat every week. Welcome to a new world—*said to Brian Bosworth, after he graduated from college (and college football) to join the Seattle Seahawks.*

1033   Without her, nothing would be possible—*referring to his wife.*

1034   Six moves, six complete changes of life and not once had she known where she was going—*referring to his wife and job changes as coach.*

1035   Winners bring reality up to their vision. Losers lower their vision down to reality.

1036   The really great football coaches—Lombardi, Paul Brown, Don Shula, Blanton Collier—all have been great teachers. Being great teachers, they've been great motivators. They had the capacity to take an individual and take him further, improve him and upgrade his performance level more than any other coach possibly could.

1037   People get the impression that "mistake-free football" is computer football, which isn't the case at all. It is based on a philosophy that if we can eliminate our own mistakes in practice as much as possible, by constantly reviewing the basic alignments we'll see in each game, then we're going to reduce our chances for error.

1038   Repeated actions are stored as habits and if the repeated actions aren't sound, then what comes out in a game can't be sound. What comes out will be bad habits.

1039   We stand there watching and watching and it seems like the ball is in the air forever. And it's good. It's good. How can it be good? I don't know but it was good. A 63-yard field goal. A record that still stands. Game's over and we lose—*said when Detroit lost to the New Orleans Saints in 1970 when Tom Dempsey kicked game-winning field goal on last play of game. Knox was a Detroit assistant coach.*

1040   The way I see it, you first become head coaching material when your players start imitating you and making fun of your mannerisms behind your back.

1041   You can buy a father, but never the mother—*referring to recruiting.*

1042   Talk to a kid like he's already at your school—*referring to a recruiting technique.*

1043   If you were a good recruiter, it meant you later had to be a good baby sitter.

1044   Pass blocking is an alley fight. I still tell my linemen to think of themselves as the only person between the defender and a loved one.

1045   If nothing else, I think selling used cars helped me appreciate offensive linemen. Nobody wants their job, but everybody needs them to get around.

1046   The more somebody wants something, the more he will pay. Thus, if what he wants belongs to you, the more you should ask.

1047   The more one man earns, the better it is for all men.

1048   I will never fault a player for trying to get more money.

1049   The bean counter thinks getting the job done cheaper is better than getting the job done right.

1050   I've survived as a coach by giving everybody the benefit of the doubt. But once there is doubt, there are no more benefits.

1051   When you give, you receive. That's a philosophy that transcends religion.

1052   I yell at my players, sure, but it's always constructive yelling.

1053   The only thing you can ask any man to do is his best.

Joseph L. "Joe" Kuharich

Coach: University of San Francisco 1948–1951, Chicago Cardinals 1952, Washington Redskins 1954–1958, Notre Dame 1959–1962, Philadelphia Eagles 1964–1968. Record: 100-118-3.

1054   The charge on that blocked kick came either from the inside or the outside.

1055   Trading quarterbacks is rare but not unusual.

1056   I'm not vacillating you. I can only answer a question about a conclusive.

1057   We were three points behind, but that's not the same as being even.

1058   A missed block here, a missed assignment there, it all adds up — *referring to losing game, 56–7.*

1059   They say you can't win them all. I say sometimes you can't win one—*said during his first year coaching the Eagles, when his team lost its first ten games.*

1060   They never felt his speed until he was gone.

Frank J. Kush

Coach: Arizona State 1958–1979, Hamilton Tiger-Cats (CFL) 1981, Baltimore/Indianapolis Colts 1982–1984 (team moved after 1983 season), Arizona Outlaws (USFL) 1985. Record: 206-96-3.

1061   Today the three R's in football are recruiting, revenue and recognition.

1062   I never punched the kid—*said after Kevin Rutledge claimed Kush hit him during game on October 28, 1978, leading to the end of the coach's association with Arizona State.*

1063   After 25 years they took me and threw me out like an old washrag—*said after accused of striking player; he resigned.*

1064   I've been asked by people a lot of times, "Is this the highlight of your career?" When we went to a bowl they asked, when we beat Nebraska they asked, when I was coach of the year they asked. Every time I've given the same answer. Like hell it is. Something else will always come up that's just as enjoyable or better.

Earl L. "Curly" Lambeau

Coach: Green Bay Packers 1921–1949, Chicago Cardinals 1950–1951, Washington Redskins 1952–1953. Record: 231-133-23.

1065   Mr. Peck, I've been talking to some of the other young fellows and we think we could get together a football team. It will be a great thing for Green Bay and the company. Will you back us?—*said in 1919 to Frank Peck, president of Indian Packing Co. of Green Bay, who gave $500.*

1066   The lid's off, boys, but stay out of jail—*meaning, have a drink after the game.*

1067   The surprise plan is we're going to run the ball at them all day.

1068   Run them to death.

Thomas W. "Tom" Landry

Coach: Dallas Cowboys 1960–1988. Record: 271-180-6.

1069   Without my faith, I'd be in real bad shape. Faith gives a man hope and hope is what life is all about.

1070   My own purpose is to serve God in whatever capacity He wants me to serve Him.

1071   We're tough because we've got to be tough to play pro football. But if we see a man hurt, we don't kick him. We pick him up.

1072   There are many outstanding Christian people in pro football.

1073   I simply believe that Christ wanted me to bring Him into my daily life, including football.

1074   Religion is anything but passive.

1075   You know, I think I said a four-letter word.

1076   I can't wait to see if we can overcome our troubles.

1077   When something exciting happens and the fans see me showing no emotion, they think I'm crazy, I'm sure.

1078   During exciting games, it's easy to get carried away, to let emotions grab you. But I believe in being in control.

1079   The reason I don't do a song and dance during games is that I'm concentrating so intensely. That's how you can get two or three plays ahead of the team itself. That's how you win.

1080   Leadership is a matter of having people look at you and gain confidence seeing how you react. If you're in control, they're in control. It's not that I'm unemotional or computerized. But as a coach I seldom see a play as others do. If it's a pass play, I'm trying to read the opposing team's pass defense. I usually don't even see the ball in the air. If it's a running play, I'm looking at the point of attack—where the key block is. I have to know whether a play broke down because of our blocking or because the other team changed its defense. If you were to see me as a cheerleader, that would mean I was only watching instead of thinking.

1081   If you win a football game, you teach. If you lose, you learn.

1082   On defense you have to accept the fact that you're going to give the other guy the first shot. The initial advantage is his.

1083   I think defensive coaching is more exciting to me than offensive because you can never predict what the opposing offense is going to do, and you're at a disadvantage from the start.

1084   I was delighted it was his head and not his knee—*said after quarterback Roger Staubach suffered slight concussion.*

1085   We have no play where Roger is supposed to run. He runs enough—*referring to Roger Staubach.*

1086   This is the toughest part of the business. This is the only part of this business I don't really like very much. Today I had to make a decision. I had to cut a fine young man, a good friend, a good Christian.

1087   You have to remember that football players are human beings with human feelings, not slabs of beef or robots.

1088   The heat is entirely mental. It's only when you pass out that it becomes physical.

1089   It was terrible out there, terrible for both sides. That, in itself, made this game distinctive from any other—*said after his team lost to Packers in January '68 championship game played in 14 below zero weather.*

1090   Before Brown, coaching staffs weren't very big or organized. He introduced classroom techniques and written tests and statistical studies because he thought of himself as a teacher—*referring to Paul Brown.*

1091   His attention to detail turned coaching into a full-time profession—*referring to Paul Brown.*

1092   He would never hand players beautiful computer books like we do today. He made them write every detail of every block, every move of every play in their notebooks until they couldn't forget their assignments—*referring to Paul Brown.*

1093   Teamwork is the ability to have different thoughts about things. It's the ability to argue and stand up and say loud and strong what you feel. But in the end it's also the ability to adjust to what is best for the team.

1094   A clique to me is a group that is at odds with another group.

1095   That's one way to look at it. The other is that I haven't had a promotion in 21 years—*reply in 1981 when someone said he had been the only coach in Dallas' history.*

1096   This isn't my party. It's the team's party—*referring to a party in celebration of his signing a long-term coaching contract.*

1097   You don't build character without somebody slapping you around.

1098   Achievement builds character. People striving, being knocked down and coming back ... that's what builds character in a man.

1099   The player without character usually finds excuses for why he shouldn't produce with everything he has. A player with character looks for the best in every situation. There's always hope for him even when the clock is running out. He's looking for a play to win the game.

1100   A team that has character doesn't need stimulation.

1101   A lot of young people really never had to struggle for anything in their lives. When it finally happens, the character isn't there to get them through. What do they turn to? Alcohol, drugs ... you name it.

1102   I admire a man with courage.

1103   I never got a chance to show them my personal feelings because I controlled their careers, their success.

1104   My job is more than just winning but also dealing, in a way, with people's lives.

1105   It's an injustice to the players to get too close to them. Subconsciously he'll tend to use that as a crutch.

1106   I have to make decisions affecting players' lives. I can't avoid situations where players may dislike me for a decision I had to make. They may dislike me even though that decision might have been a right one.

1107   Secretly, I guess, I'd love to get close to my players.

1108   Perhaps if there has been one failing within our organization over the years, it is that we haven't tried to dispel the notion that our success comes out of a computer. It doesn't. It comes out of the sweat glands of our coaches and players.

1109   Achieving goals, which really means winning in some form, is the ultimate in a man's life.

1110   If he was successful he was very outgoing, very emotional. If he was unsuccessful he wasn't speaking to anybody. He had moods—*said of Vince Lombardi when both were working as assistant coaches of the New York Giants.*

1111   I planned to be in business. That's why I took my industrial management degree. I was in business in Houston during the off-season. I was constantly preparing for business while I was finishing up what I thought was just going to be an assistant's coaching job. Then, about the time I was ready to step down as coach and go into business, that's when the Dallas job opened up. I was living in Texas anyway. It was a natural transition. But I hadn't even thought about it before.

1112   I think a player should have great freedom of expression. My criterion is when it starts bothering the team and its effectiveness then I'll do something about it.

1113   Whether they spike the ball or do this or that. It's something that's part of our time now. We deal with it as best we can.

1114   Players talk about individualism, but I believe they all want to live and work under a single standard.

1115   We'll put up with someone who won't conform as long as he gets the job done. But we can't get along with a player who doesn't get the job done or conform, either.

1116   We just have to have patience—*referring to dealing with trouble-some Duane Thomas.*

1117   That was a unique case—*referring to the preferential treatment he gave to Duane Thomas in 1971, when the Cowboys went to the Super Bowl.*

1118   You couldn't expect a team to go through that again—*referring to fact that Duane Thomas didn't play for the Cowboys in 1972.*

1119   The key is discipline. Without it there is no morale.

1120   No one wants any restraints. But no one is really free unless he has certain boundaries to operate within.

1121   A team must have the ability to believe in each other.

1122   Does that tell you how far we've fallen?—*referring to the cover photo on an issue of the* Dallas Cowboy Weekly—*a cheerleader instead of a player.*

1123   You win a play-off game and it means you're the best team on a given day.

1124   Keep your comments to yourself when you're talking to the press. Teams are just going to use what you say against you.

1125   The insecurity of this business makes you feel like you must fight so hard, give up so much.

1126   Nothing funny ever happens on a football field.

1127   Football is still primarily emotion. Hitting comes first. Thinking comes second.

1128   A lot of good men with head coaching potential are destroyed in poor situations. They couldn't display their talents, were fired and never came back.

1129   This game is rougher than I thought—*referring to tennis.*

1130   I go to training camp every year scared to death. That keeps me on edge.

1131   I do feel more at ease with myself. I don't know whether it's because I've gotten older or that my faith has improved.

1132   I think the older you get the more you enjoy life. Certain things don't seem as important as they once did. . . . Now I don't get so hung up on perfection, on people doing things perfectly.

1133   You look for perfection and you'll be disappointed. . . .

1134   If the play succeeds, he should get a thrill out of it. If it's intercepted, I'll get a thrill out of it—*reply to fact that opposing coach, Don Shula, might use play suggested by President Nixon in Super Bowl VI.*

1135   I'm not sure whether it was the greatest game ever played, but there's no question . . . that it marked the time, the game and the place where pro football really caught on, where the public attention was aroused and brought the game into the spotlight—*referring to game where Colts beat Giants 23–17 in overtime for the championship, December 28, 1958. Landry was assistant Giant coach.*

1136   There are many successful philosophies because there are many successful coaches.

1137   You've got to have a clear-cut philosophy to be successful and it must be transmitted to your players. They must thoroughly understand everything you are trying to do, so much so that eventually it simply becomes instinctive to them.

1138   A lot of winning is tradition.

1139   I don't look at past records because they mean nothing.

1140   You can't give up because you never know what's going to happen.

1141   We always wanted to be imaginative. I've never believed the game depends only on personnel. I think strategy counts, try to outflank the other coach. That means we've made mistakes—daring teams do—but it means we weren't boring either.

1142   Our defense is designed to stop any play along the line of scrimmage. At least, that's the theory.

1143   Being a successful coach often is nothing more than the belief you have in a player—that he can do it.

1144   To get men to do what they don't want to do in order to achieve what they want to achieve. That's what coaching is all about.

1145   If it ever comes to the point in our society where it doesn't make any difference whether women go into the locker room, then football no longer will make any difference nor will newspapers because everything will have gone down the drain. There are some things you don't do and this is one of them.

1146   The more success you have, the more people would like to see you fail.

1147   Sooner or later, you've got to go down.

1148   If you are in this business long enough, you will see the downside of the NFL. It just seems like it is one of those years.

1149   I certainly don't put all my life in winning football games.

1150   I'm not bitter at all—*said after being fired in 1989.*

Elmer F. Layden

Coach: Loras 1925–1926, Duquesne 1927–1933, Notre Dame 1934–1940. Record: 103-34-11.

1151   Three of my better linemen on the 1929 team—Sammy Pratt, Moko Lesser and Leo Silverstein—would not show up for the West Virginia game because it fell on Yom Kippur. The priests who ran Duquesne were not in the business of letting color or creed get in the way of education.

1152   Unlike today's coaches, we got dressed up for a game. Coaches today sort of pride themselves on looking sloppy. They wear all kinds of sweatshirts, old pants and baseball caps, whereas in my time, we dressed up. I remember one season at Duquesne when I wore a black Chesterfield overcoat, white silk scarf and black derby hat on the cold days.

1153   To my shock, one of my stars, Bill Shakespeare, was having trouble with English—*referring to a student at Notre Dame.*

1154   The fundamentals are what we stressed, blocking and tackling. You can cook up all the fancy plays you want as a coach, but they won't amount to anything unless your boys can block and tackle.

1155   During cold weather, Brue served hot bouillon. Not until 1968 did I learn that he and Doc O'Donnell spiked it with a half-gallon of wine. "On those cold days, we sure had a spirited team in the second half," Brue says.

1156   There may have been some seats along the field, but nobody used them. The spectators followed the teams up and down the field. "They were practically selling popcorn in our backfield," is the way I described it afterwards—*referring to game versus Washington & Jefferson, 1928.*

1157   The dressing room was a shed at one end of the field, and even if my oratory did arouse the team, it wouldn't have taken much to knock down the door—*referring to same game as above.*

1158   Doggo Burns was put on the sideline without a headgear. He was told to stay near the head linesman and be inconspicuous. The way the crowd milled up and down the sidelines, this instruction was unnecessary. After returning the kickoff, our team went right into formation and the quarterback, Ganzy Benedict, threw a long pass to Burns, whom nobody had noticed missing as we had lined up. He caught it and we were inside the W & J 20-yard line—*referring to same game.*

1159   The package I could offer these boys consisted of tuition and room and board in return for playing football and working at a part-time job. Their room really was a cot in the gymnasium until basketball season began. After that, they were relegated to a loft above the main building; or, if they were especially lucky, Dean Muldoon might put them up in his apartment. Many of these youngsters came from the coal fields of Pennsylvania. They had no desire to follow their dads into the mines. They left home with the clothes on their backs and little else. They were not expected to return, and Duquesne was their last stop in search of three square meals and an opportunity to keep away from the mines.

Francis W. "Frank" Leahy

Coach: Boston College 1939–1940, Notre Dame 1941–1943 and 1946–1953. Record: 107-13-9.

1160   To me, it was a sacred trust—*referring to coaching at Notre Dame.*

1161   There is no difference to me between serving Our Lady and winning a football team.

1162   Leon Hart, Leon Hart, you do not deserve to represent Our Lady.... Will someone give Leon 76 cents for meal money and let him start hitchhiking for home right now? I see absolutely no need for his mortal soul. Let us now bow our heads and pray to Our Lady for forgiveness, for we have disgraced her terribly—*said during halftime of game against North Carolina, which was tied 6–6. Notre Dame went on to win 42–6.*

1163   Remember, young men of Notre Dame, that a tie is the same as a defeat when you play for Our Lady. Let me recall a line from that most stirring of songs, the Notre Dame Victory march. The words entreat us to "Shake down the thunder from the sky." This afternoon, you play Army. You must redeem the honor of our school, which has suffered. Now I ask you, in the sacred name of Our Lady, to go onto that field and "Shake down the thunder." Go and persevere, Our Lady demands it!

1164   Lads, you're not to miss practice unless your parents died or you died.

1165   Egotism is the anesthetic that lulls the pain of stupidity.

1166   No coach can permit himself to be altered by changing times.

1167   A coach shapes lives.

1168   I raised the threshold of pain that some young men had and I taught them to work harder.

1169   There are no shortcuts in life, only those which we imagine.

1170   I could not believe that Our Lady wanted anything less than perfection.

1171   Unless you have total commitment to excellence, you have a flawed attitude toward life.

1172   There is a point where competitiveness ends and fanaticism begins.

1173   We did not win football games for Our Lady by loving the opposition. Rather we sought to find respect for ourselves.

1174   I want the eleven most savage men to play for me.

1175   I run the house much like a football team. About once every two weeks I line the children up and grade them on five points—neatness, courtesy, respectfulness, cooperation and unselfishness.

1176   We have eight children and we want more. I was never one to hold down the score, you know.

1177   A fullback, I hope. That would be excellent because we might be weak at that position in 18 years—*said when his wife gave birth to a boy, their sixth child.*

1178   A spoonful of humor makes the serious message go down easier.

1179   I want an "Alma Mater Clause"—*said when he signed a five-year coaching contract with Boston College because, "If Notre Dame (his alma mater) should ever call me, I would want to be free."*

1180   My meager vocabulary lacks the words to describe fittingly the monumental feeling of joy which permeated my entire body and soul—*said about his feelings after he was asked if he'd be interested in coaching Notre Dame.*

1181   I am a preacher of old fashioned virtues.

1182   Joseph, oh Joseph, you are aware that I attempt to avoid profanity, with the exception of an occasional "hell" or "damn." That is true, is it not? Joseph, please forgive the use of the unpleasant expletive. At the moment, it is the only word that seems to fit. Joseph, we got fucked—*said in the midst of a bad season after a game in which the referees made some bad calls against his team.*

1183   When two great teams meet, defense tends to dominate.

1184   I believe you can win every game on your schedule if you are willing to pay the price.

1185   Upsets are part of football's nature. The first law of competition is never to underestimate the opponent.

1186   Playing the game of life without God as your coach is like riding on a ship without a captain, without a crew and without a rudder in the middle of the ocean.

1187   It is my firm conviction that a heavy concentration of Irish is not conducive to tranquility.

1188   Coaching burns out a man's insides.

1189   I owed it to my family to resign while I was still alive.

1190   I used to be—*reply to woman who asked the sick and elderly coach, "Aren't you Frank Leahy?"*

1191   Those speeches are all I have left—*said after he had retired from coaching and was suffering from leukemia, arthritis, heart problems and more.*

1192   Because he is head coach of Notre Dame. And I used to be—*reply to why he was jealous of Ara Parseghian.*

1193   Only 11 men can be on the field at the same time. Every other student is the 12th man.

Marvin D. "Marv" Levy

Coach: University of New Mexico 1958–1959, University of California 1960–1963, William & Mary 1964–1968, Montreal Alouettes (CFL) 1973–1977, Kansas City Chiefs 1978–1982, Chicago Blitz (USFL) 1984, Buffalo Bills 1986– . Record: 150-172-9.

1194   I don't want to put on a three-piece suit, stuff a bunch of papers into a briefcase, go down to court and worry about legalisms instead of justice—*referring to why he dropped out of Harvard Law School.*

1195   I think it made me more palatable to the faculty, which is always suspect of the role intercollegiate football plays—*referring to William & Mary and the fact that he graduated Phi Beta Kappa from Coe College.*

1196   They don't go hand in hand, but frequently the bright and smart person is a person of good character.

1197   I wasn't ready to settle down and be professorial—*referring to reason why he left William & Mary to join the Philadelphia Eagles as assistant coach.*

1198   People expect too much from rookies; rookies don't expect enough of themselves.

1199   We want to strike a balance between the run and pass. And over the past 20 years, I think you would find that 300-yard plus games have been lost more than won because you get an imbalance.

1200   There's three parts to football: offense, defense and special teams. You'd no more ignore special teams than you would offense or defense.

1201   I have a saying, "What you do speaks so loudly, no one can hear what you say."

1202   I'll give you a bunch of rules but there's really only three that matter: work hard, be on time and be a good citizen.

1203   You over-officious jerk!—*said to a referee.*

1204   There's no such thing as momentum going into the playoffs.

1205   I'd go to one luncheon on Wednesday and another on Thursday and I had to play Southern Cal on Saturday. Two things I learned out there: never go to those booster club dinners and skip lunches—*referring to coaching at the University of California at Berkeley.*

1206   Every season wears on me.

1207   You're going to have problems. You deal with them. You seek to solve them. That's part of coaching.

1208   I am tired of what have become the same inane questions—*referring to sportswriters.*

1209   We have liberated Paris, but it's 600 miles to Berlin ... I'll be on the injury list for strained analogy next week—*referring to the long road to the Super Bowl after clinching the AFC East championship in 1988.*

Louis L. "Lou" Little

Coach: Georgetown 1924–1929, Columbia University 1930–1956. Record: 151-128-13.

1210   I want men who will knock the other fellow's brains out, then help him up and brush him off.

1211   Don't you know better than to pay attention to me when I'm mad.

1212   Their primary purpose in college is academic development. Football must be subordinate to that purpose.

1213   I never did anything for you boys. You did everything for me.

Vincent T. "Vince" Lombardi

Coach: Green Bay Packers 1959–1967, Washington Redskins 1969. Record: 106-36-6.

1214   Winning isn't everything ... it's the only thing.

1215   Fatigue makes cowards of us all.

1216   The will to excel and the will to win, they endure. They are more important than any events that occasion them.

1217   I went to the men's room and I was standing there at the urinal and I get a tap on the shoulder and this guy's standing there with a placemat and a pen asking me for my autograph. He said he didn't want to bother me while I was having lunch.

1218   I've never known a man worth his salt who in the long run, deep down in his heart, didn't appreciate the grind, the discipline. There is something in good men that really yearns for discipline.

1219   The good Lord gave you a body that can stand most anything. It's your mind you have to convince.

1220   Things are either just wonderful or just terrible.

1221   Hell, I'm an emotional man. I cry . . . I'm not ashamed of crying. Football's an emotional game. You can't be a cold fish and go out and coach. If you're going to be involved in it, you gotta take your emotions with you.

1222   I'm tired of making chicken salad out of chicken shit.

1223   I hate people to use bad language but God damn it, I'm awful during football season.

1224   They call it coaching, but it is teaching. You do not just tell them it is so. You show them the reasons why it is so, and then you repeat and repeat until they are convinced, until they know.

1225   I have been called a tyrant, but I have also been called the coach of the simplest system in football and I suppose there is some truth in both.

1226   You can't run a football team if you have to go to this committee for that and that committee for this.

1227   I have been hired to do a job without interference, and I don't expect to have any.

1228   One thing I won't stand for is a player standing at a public bar. I don't care if he's drinking ginger ale and talking to a friend, it just doesn't look good if a fan sees him in the place.

1229   I know it was ginger ale, because after he left, I tasted it—*said after he reduced fine from $500 to $300 after he caught a player drinking at a bar.*

1230   Don't ask questions you can answer yourself.

1231   Success is like a narcotic. One becomes addicted to it, but it has a terrible side to it because it saps the elation of the victory and deepens the despair of defeat.

1232   If you can't take my pressure, then for sure you can't take it in a game.

1233   To play this game, you must have that fire in you, and there is nothing that stokes that fire like hate.

1234   I believe a coach must be a pedagogue. He has to pound the lessons into the players by rote, the same way you teach pupils in the classroom.

1235   Pro football . . . is a violent, dangerous sport. To play it other than violently would be imbecile.

1236   There shall be weeping and gnashing of teeth.

1237   I'll do all the thinking. Just do exactly as I tell you. I'll take the responsibility. Don't improvise.

1238   Coaches who can outline plays on a blackboard are a dime a dozen. The ones who win get inside their players and motivate them.

1239   Practice doesn't make perfect. Perfect practice makes perfect.

1240   I'll tell you this, mister, you're going to play Sunday if we have to carry you out on a stretcher—*said to a Redskin who hurt his ankle during practice.*

1241   I asked the team to win this one for me. I told them I'd never ask them for this again. But I will.

1242   We never won as many as I wanted to—which was all of them.

1243   When you win you get a feeling of exhilaration. When you lose you get a feeling of resolution. You resolve never to lose again.

1244   Now go through that door and bring back a victory.

1245   To be a good coach, you have to be the opposite of what you feel. When your team is going bad, you want to get on their ass but that's when everybody else is on their ass. Their family, their friends, the fans, the media, the guy in the grocery store. That's when you need to pat them on the back, to tell them to just keep working hard and everything will be all right. Conversely, when everything is going good, you don't have to pat them on the back because everybody else is. That's when you have to be tough.

1246   I believe that a man who's late for meetings or for the bus won't run his pass routines right. He'll be sloppy.

1247   No prima donnas. No special treatment. No pets.

1248   The greatest glory is not in never falling but in rising every time we fall.

1249   Your eyes are dull. Have you been masturbating, mister?

1250   Drag him off the field and let's get on with the scrimmage— *referring to Bob Long, who hurt self in preseason—torn cartilage.*

1251   I've found out the challenge in something is not maintaining it, but attaining it.

1252   I've got to have men who bend to me.

1253   All I want to know is how far can I push a guy.

1254   Nobody wants to be told they're making errors, not the way I tell them.

1255   Otto, if you want to survive in pro football as a head coach, you have to be a son of a bitch 100 percent of the time— *advice to Otto Graham, former Browns quarterback who became coach of Washington Redskins.*

1256   How did I do out there?— *question to coaches after he raised hell with men out on the field.*

1257   What do you want to talk to the doctor about it for? The weather's beautiful. The sun is shining— *said to player worried about frostbite during championship game played with temperature 14 below zero.*

1258   We went for a touchdown instead of a field goal because I didn't want all those freezing people up in the stands to have to sit through a sudden death— *said during same game.*

1259   Those decisions don't come from the mind. They come from the guts.

1260   If I ever hear "nigger" or "dago" or "kike" or anything like that around here, regardless of who you are, you're through with me.

1261   We make no issue over a man's color.

1262   How can you, a good Christian, feel that way?— *said to a bigot.*

1263   I don't think I can get it. My name ends in a vowel—*said after Red Blaik left coaching job at Army and the school was looking for a replacement.*

1264   I'll tell you this is the last goddamn Jew I'm going to vote for. And only because he's replacing another Jew. You get too many of those sons of bitches and you got a problem—*said after he approved Leonard Tose as owner of the Philadelphia Eagles. Tose and others bought team from Jerry Wolman in spring of 1969.*

1265   These men have something more than respect for each other. There is love on this ball club.

1266   I don't think there's a city in the country to compare with what New York has to offer.

1267   When you're with the team, you'll eat what the team eats—*said to his wife, who asked for ice cream when the team was eating pie at a team dinner. She was the only woman there.*

1268   The great thing about Marie is that she knocks me down when I'm up and she picks me up when I'm down—*referring to his wife.*

1269   You'll make a lot of mistakes in your life, Susan, but if you learn from every mistake, you really didn't make a mistake—*said to his daughter.*

1270   I say emphatically—we are not an old football team. We have experience—and that's what you need to win in this league.

1271   You don't have to win 'em aesthetically. You win 'em the best you can.

1272   Teams do not go physically stale. They go mentally stale.

1273   I hold it more important to have the players' confidence than to have their affection.

1274   The guards are the focal point of the offense. Everything they do is critical. They open holes for the quick openers, clear the way for the sweeps, and protect the passer.

1275   On defense, a player can depend on his reactions, without thinking ahead, because what he does depends primarily upon what the man he is facing does. He keys upon an offensive player and he is more an instinctive player. But the offensive player has to know at all times where he is going to go and what he has to do when he gets there.

1276   The defensive player has to be tougher. Playing on instinct and reaction, he has to play with abandon. You can't be an abandoned guard or tackle on defense. You have to have discipline.

1277   Having a beer and pizza at the half. The score: Lions 8, Christians 7—*message on back of a picture postcard of the Colosseum, sent while Lombardi was touring Europe.*

1278   No leader, however great, can long continue unless he wins battles. The battle decides all.

1279   Leadership is based on a spiritual quality, the power to inspire, the power to inspire others to follow.

1280   The obvious difference between the group and the man who leads them is not in lack of strength, not in lack of knowledge, but rather in lack of will. The character, rather than education, is man's greatest need and man's greatest safeguard because character is higher than intellect.

1281   Running a football team is no different from running any other kind of organization—an army, a political party, a business. The principles are the same. The objective is to win—to beat the other guy. Maybe that sounds hard or cruel but I don't think it is. It's the reality of life that men are competitive and the most competitive games draw the most competitive men.

1282   Football teams are no different from any other groups. They are good examples of success and failure, of competence and incompetence, of inspiration and dullness.

1283   You just wait until you see me emote.

1284   I'm just going to give these guys complete hell today. No matter what happens. Because today is going to be one of those days.

1285   A game that requires the constant conjuring of animosity.

1286   A school without football is in danger of deteriorating into a medieval study hall.

1287   Winning isn't everything—but wanting to win is.

1288   Winning is a habit. Unfortunately, so is losing.

1289   You guys whip the Bears and I'll whip old man Halas' ass.

1290   Look at the suntans you're getting. Isn't that beautiful? Just like a health spa—*said to players training in 92-degree heat.*

1291   If you really want something you can have it if you are willing to pay the price. And the price means that you have to work better and harder than the next guy.

1292   Only three things should matter to you: your religion, your family and the Green Bay Packers. In that order.

1293   They may not love you at the time, but they will later—*referring to disciplining kids.*

1294   Your moral integrity is the most priceless thing you possess.

1295   Wait till we get out to practice. I dreamed up a new play. I woke up at three in the morning.

1296   How does a man meet his failures? That is the measure of the man. If he does not quit or curl up he has the right stuff in him. Be a hard loser.

1297   There is no such thing as a good loser, but in losing one can still be a good sport.

1298   He worked on me and molded me and fashioned my entire approach to the game—*referring to working under Red Blaik.*

1299   Can you imagine anybody living in a place like this? This is just the end of the world—*said when stranded by a snowstorm in a hotel in Green Bay in 1950.*

1300   This is a great life down here, but I honestly don't know how much of it I could take. If I had to stay away from work too long—well, I might not like it—*said in Miami, on vacation.*

1301   There's a great—a great closeness on a football team, a rapport between the men and the coach that's like no other sport. It's a binding together, a knitting together. For me, it's like father and sons.

1302   Tackling is more natural than blocking. If a man is running down the street with everything you own, you won't let him get away. That's tackling.

1303   A blitz is used to cover a weakness.

1304   The quicker a ball gets to the receiver, the quicker it gets back—*in other words, when punting, kick the ball high in the air.*

1305   Red, you want to be Santa Claus or you want to be a football coach? There's no room for both—*said to assistant coach who wanted time off for Christmas shopping.*

1306   Sure I think of quitting coaching. Every Tuesday after every Sunday I think of it.

1307   You don't need to play. We'll give you your salary. We'll take care of everything. You don't have to worry—*said to player who in '64 had colostomy and almost died but came back to camp the following season.*

1308   Leaders are made, they are not born. They are made by hard effort, which is the price which all of us must pay to achieve any goal that is worthwhile. In spite of what many think, none of us are really born equal, but rather unequal, and the talented have no more responsibility for their birthright than the underprivileged for theirs. The measure of each is what each does in a specific situation.

1309   Mental toughness is spartanism with its qualities of sacrifice and self-denial, dedication, fearlessness and love. The love I'm speaking of is not necessarily liking or the love that a man may have for his wife. The love I'm speaking of is loyalty, which is the greatest of loves.

1310   Championships are won on defense.

1311   The word "selflessness" as opposed to "selfishness" is what I try to teach.

1312   If you can bring down their best man, it's all over.

1313   You are foolish if you don't go at a team's weakness.

1314   This is a game for madmen. In football we are all mad.

1315   The woods are full of performers. I want champions.

1316   Am I like this? Am I really like this?—*said after reading an article about himself.*

1317   How would you like to live with him?—*said by Mrs. Marie Lombardi.*

1318   In coaching you speak in clichés. But I mean every one of them.

1319   I have such a terrible temper. It's the only way I can keep it under control—*referring to going to Mass daily.*

1320   I meant to make him mad, but I didn't mean to make him that mad—*said after player told him "Get off my back or get yourself another fullback."*

1321   You can't face them, you don't know how to tell him, but you do—*referring to cutting a veteran.*

1322   Football's still just a blocking and tackling game.

1323   Men want to follow. It gives them security to know there is someone who cares enough to chew them out a little bit or correct their mistakes.

1324   The harder you work, the harder it is to surrender.

1325   Everybody loves a gambler until he loses.

1326   You've got to win the war with the man in front of you.

1327   I never go into any game without feeling we can win. And I go into every one scared.

1328   So where does that leave Pope John?—*said after an organization voted him Italian of the Year, 1961.*

1329   Mental toughness is essential to success.

1330   Success demands singleness of purpose.

1331   You will find the extent of a man's determination on the goal line.

1332   Confidence is contagious. So is lack of confidence.

1333   I demand a commitment to excellence and to victory and that is what life is all about.

1334   You don't do things right once in awhile. You do them right all the time.

1335   The difference between success and failure is in energy.

1336   Any man's finest hour is when he has worked his heart out, exhausted on the field of battle, victorious.

1337   I miss the fire on Sunday—*referring to why he took coaching job with the Redskins.*

1338   What would I do over again if I were given the chance? Good question. I guess I would pray for more patience and understanding.

1339   You can mean a lot to mine if you pray for me—*said by a hospitalized, dying Lombardi to a player who said, "You meant a lot to my life."*

Donald "Don" McCafferty

Coach: Baltimore Colts 1970–1972, Detroit Lions 1973. Record: 32-18-1.

1340   When I first took over here, someone asked me what I'd do about the players who wore beards and long hair and wacky clothes. I told him that styles change and I was ready to go along with those changes.

1341   Some coaches are hollerers, some aren't. It's just not in my makeup. Who's to say what's best? Is Bud Grant a yeller? Is Weeb Ewbank? No, I save my yelling for the officials—when they deserve it.

Daniel E. "Dan" McGugin

Coach: Vanderbilt 1904–1917 and 1919–1934. Record: 197-55-19.

1342   In that cemetery sleep your grandfathers and down on that field are the grandsons of the damn Yankees who put them there—*said before game with Michigan.*

1343   You are about to be put to an ordeal which will show the stuff that's in you.

1344   How you fight is what you will be remembered by. If any shirks, the Lord pity him. He will be downgraded in the hearts of the rest of you as long as he lives.

1345   Now is there any man here who will not fight every inch of the way? Will any man here disgrace himself and live in the contempt of his teammates the rest of his days?

1346   With each one of you boys there was a time—you knew nothing about it, of course—a time when you were two months old, or five months, when your mother looked at you in the cradle and she wondered, she asked herself, what kind of heart beat in that little body; of how this boy, as he grew into a man, would meet his first real test of courage; whether, when that time came, she could feel the pride that only a mother can feel for a son who is courageous—and fearless—or whether there might, perhaps, have to be a different feeling. She knew that such a time, such a day, would come. Today, she may be wondering...

1347   No reputable coach nowadays signals nor sends in players to carry messages.

John H. McKay

Coach: University of Southern California 1960–1975, Tampa Bay Buccaneers 1976–1984. Record: 172-131-9.

1348   I'd like to have won by 2,000 points—*referring to team's attempt to score a last minute touchdown despite 30–21 lead.*

1349   Football is one of the greatest sports in the world because it's so much like a chess match. It's more a coach's game than most. There's more that can be planned and less that is improvised on the field than in other sports.

1350   The cold weather didn't seem to bother him in 1966 when he beat us, 51–0—*reply to Ara Parseghian's comment, "The cold weather seems to thicken the blood or something," after Southern Cal beat Notre Dame, 55–24, in 1974.*

1351   You can't play with big heavy linemen. You must have speed on the outside, speed on the inside.

1352   As soon as one game is over, you begin to worry about the next one. As soon as one season is over, the same thing happens.

1353   The more I win, the more I can't stand the thought of losing.

1354   During the season every moment I'm awake is devoted to football. Everything else I enjoy—my family, golf, movies—is out.

1355   Coaching is very lonely, because one man alone is responsible for the team.

1356   Nobody knows what it's like to be a head football coach, unless he is one.

1357   All players can't perform equally, but they can all give the same effort. My rule is: if you've given a player hell, tell him you still love him.

1358   Father, it serves you right for hiring a Presbyterian—*said to a priest associated with Notre Dame, after USC beat them. The losers' coach was Ara Parseghian.*

1359   No matter where you go the rest of your lives, you will remember you played in this game—*pep talk before important USC-Notre Dame game.*

1360   A genius in the National Football League is a guy who won last week.

1361   As soon as a coach begs, "Please, please play for me," he becomes a whore. Don't play hard for me. Play hard for yourself. If you don't want to, fine. But if we lose, don't come sobbing to me.

1362   Does a team have to be emotional to win? Well, I've always said nobody is more emotional than Corky and she can't play football worth a damn—*referring to his wife.*

1363   A runner must understand that there's one bad thing about carrying that football—it attracts a crowd.

1364   Training rules must be honored because if a player cannot make a sacrifice off the field, he is very likely to find it more difficult on the field, especially in the fourth quarter of a tight game.

1365   It's obvious you're not going to win this game for yourselves. In that case, would you consider winning it for the coaching staff's eight wives and 23 children?—*said during halftime talk when team was losing. It went on to tie the game.*

1366   College administrators have complained that we're just a farm system for the pros. But less than three percent of all college players turn professional.

1367   There can't be a better rallying point for a university than football. It draws the alumni back to see what's going on. Why do they always have homecoming during football season?

1368   The money made from football may sound like a small fortune but you must remember it has to support all the other sports we have that generate little or no income.

1369   If you can pinpoint it, you can correct it.

1370   We knew he kicked it low, so we just put the tallest guys we had in there on defense. We told the kids it wasn't so important that they bust through and make him rush the kick as it was just getting to the scrimmage line and raising their arms high. I call that brilliant coaching—*referring to stopping a place kicker.*

1371   He's the best runner I ever ruined—*referring to Sam Cunningham, USC player, whom he turned into a defensive blocker.*

1372   O.J. is not in a union. He can carry the ball as many times as we want him to—*referring to O.J. Simpson.*

1373   Nonsense, the figures are wildly out of line. Actually, I'm going to Tampa for the cigars—*referring to reason why he left USC to coach the Tampa Bay Buccaneers.*

1374   Ho-hum. Another dynasty—*said after Tampa Bay, an expansion team, won first exhibition game after three straight losses before the start of Tampa's first season in NFL.*

1375   We will be back, maybe not in this century, but we will be back—*referring to Tampa Bay Buccaneers' first season as an expansion team in the NFL, 1976, when they lost all their games.*

1376   I'll probably take a little time off and go hide someplace—*referring to the end of his first season with Tampa Bay.*

1377   I'm in favor of it—*reply to question, "What about the Bucs' execution?"*

1378   The money thing is a helluva distraction in this business. Just sitting down to talk is a major undertaking.

1379   If we went on the road we could only take 48 players. We took 48 to Notre Dame—and a 250-piece marching band. Tell me how that saved money?

1380   I checked my heart. I didn't have one.

1381   There's nothing you can do to try and become a head coach. Nothing. Just work hard and be in the right place at the right time. It's unfortunate that our profession is not one in which you can take an examination and move up.

1382   Recruiting is a very difficult job. Except for losing, it's the worst thing about college coaching.

1383   If I were an ordinary parent trying to help my son choose a college, I would first assess his skills, find out what he wanted to do, and if I knew anything about football, look at the offense the team is using. If my son is a split receiver, for example, he shouldn't play for a wishbone team, because they never pass. Then I would tell him to study the various schools and see if they can offer him the degree he's interested in. And, as we studied each other, I'd ask, what is the coach's record? What has he accomplished? What kind of man is he?

1384   I paid his bills for a long time. After 18 years he owed me something—*said after McKay's son, Johnny, decided to attend USC.*

1385   There is nothing mysterious about developing a good team, because coaching is nothing more than teaching. Head coaches coach assistants, and then assistants impart the techniques to the players.

1386   We don't beat people with surprises but with execution.

1387   There are so many little techniques which are important that the average fan never sees from the stands. For example, how far apart do your backs stand? What spot should they take off from? Which direction should they go? What is the right stance? What is the timing of the pitchout from the quarterback to the ballcarrier?

1388   We don't use alumni too often. They just don't know the rules; something always seems to get lost in the translation—*said of recruiting.*

1389   God's busy. They have to make do with me—*reply when asked if his team prayed for victory.*

1390   I don't think he's got much of a future here. I plan on being at most of the games—*said after a player remarked he didn't do well in practice because he got nervous knowing McKay was watching him.*

1391   When I first became USC's head coach, the oldest of my four children, Michele, was only seven. Critical remarks made by newspapers and by the public were picked up by other children and repeated to my children. This happens with the sons and daughters of all coaches, and we know there are no crueler people in the world than young kids.

1392   When you notice that a team hasn't lost, check its schedule.

1393   You can't beat experience because mental mistakes beat you more than physical mistakes—in any sport.

1394   The way some coaches talk you would think no one can be any good unless he plays football. That eliminates half the people in the world. Half of them are women.

1395   Consider what Ara Parseghian did in 1964, his first year at Notre Dame. He went 9–1 with the same personnel that had a 2–7 record the previous season. He took John Huarte, a quarterback who had sat on the bench for two years, and made him the Heisman Trophy winner. Ara had the same players, no bigger, no faster than the year before.

DeOrmond "Tuss" McLaughry

Coach: Westminster 1916–1918 and 1921, Amherst 1922–1925, Brown 1926–1940, Dartmouth 1941–1942 and 1945–1954. Record: 140-143-13.

1396   In those days you could sit on a 7–0 lead, and I just let the 11 stay in there and do the job. When we went to Dartmouth the next week and the same 11 men played all the way again as we won, 10–0, the papers started calling us "The Iron Men." That was okay with me because I think it gave my men a morale boost.

Alvin N. "Bo" McMillin

Coach: Centenary (Louisiana) 1922–1924, Geneva (PA) 1925–1927, Kansas State 1928–1933, University of Indiana 1934–1947, Detroit Lions 1948–1950, Philadelphia Eagles 1951. Record: 204-111-17.

1397   You can be tough as nails and still be gentlemen.

1398   Well, I'll be a dirty name—*said to avoid swearing.*

1399   You gotta have the horses.

1400   I'm not going down there to run a graveyard—*said when he left Kansas State to coach a weak team at the University of Indiana.*

1401   I've seen a sicker cat than Indiana get well—*said at same time.*

1402   You got to ship, haul and drive.

1403   They might beat us but they won't eat us—*said of a strong rival team.*

1404   We believed in it—*referring to the power of prayer.*

John Madden

Coach: Hancock Junior College 1962–1963, Oakland Raiders 1969–1978. Record: 124-45-7.

1405   As a TV analyst, I still have football season. I think that's what most guys miss when they leave the sport.

1406   For me, TV is really an extension of coaching. My knowledge of football has come from coaching. And on TV, all I'm trying to do is pass on some of that knowledge to the viewers.

1407   The road to Easy Street goes through the sewer.

1408   I thought I was going to play football forever. That's the trouble with most good athletes.

1409   As a coach, the class that helped me the most was child psychology—*said about his student days in California.*

1410   I like Miller Lite, but some people expect me always to have a Lite in my hand. I was having breakfast once when a stranger stared at me. "Where's your Miller Lite," he said.

1411   One of the toughest things I've ever had to do was cut George Blanda during our 1976 training camp. He was about to turn 49 years old.

1412   It's not what you weigh, it's how you play.

1413   You've got to watch for what you don't want to see. You have to listen to what you don't want to hear.

1414   We were ready for it. We remembered that Ralston used that play for Stanford against Ohio State in the Rose Bowl three years ago and got away with it—*referring to Denver coach John Ralston, who tried a fake punt play but his team ran instead.*

1415   If a team becomes too old at the same time, the next step is that it becomes too young at the same time.

1416   My job is a way of life. There are no days off. To be successful, a coach must be totally dedicated. He can't own a summer cabin in the mountains or play golf in his spare time because there is no spare time.

1417   I have a very independent wife.

1418   Football should be played on God's turf, grass, in the hot sun or in freezing cold, whatever comes up that day.

1419   Almost all the women I've ever talked to about football have wanted to learn the game because of their husband or their boyfriend or their sons. I'd like to see women learn to appreciate football for themselves, not just for the males in their lives.

1420   To the TV executive, football is a TV show.

1421   In a passing offense, the idea is to force the defense to cover as much of the field as possible in order to spread it out.

1422   Even a long incomplete pass keeps a defense guessing.

1423   I've always felt that the fewer rules a coach has, the fewer rules there are for the players to break.

1424   To me, discipline in football occurs on the field, not off it. Discipline is knowing what you're supposed to do and doing it as best you can.

1425   I had only three rules on the Raiders—be on time, pay attention and play like hell when I tell you to.

1426   You're only as good as your last game and there's nothing more important than your next game.

1427   Conservative football is boring football. But when you put everything on the line on one game, teams must be conservative.

1428   Instead of playing to win, you're playing not to make the mistakes that could end up costing you the game. Execution becomes everything.

1429   The first consideration against any punt is whether you want a return or a block. It's like defending against the pass. Either you cover it tight by dropping more people into the secondary or you blitz by sending in extra rushers.

1430   If receivers are covered, a passer can do three things. He can throw the ball away, throw it in there and risk an interception, or he can get thrown for a loss, which often means losing field position. You don't want the interceptions and you don't want the loss. So Unitas did the best thing he could do. He threw it away; probably half his incompletions in that first half were that type. Those are the things that statistics don't show or that aren't understood by the fan.

1431   Watching game films, we don't eat much popcorn.

1432   Perhaps subconsciously I work every day to keep from being fired, but every day I work to do the best job I possibly can. Both mean the same thing to our organization.

1433   Football is serious.

1434   At one time we made a lot of mistakes about cutting players simply because we couldn't tell the difference between guys who didn't know what they were doing and those who couldn't do it.

1435   The way to tell the toughest sport is by how long athletes need to rest before their next appearance.

1436   Boxing is the toughest sport.

1437   When the game starts, a quarterback must be a leader, a field general. How can he be a field general if he's waiting for instructions from the bench before every play?

1438   There is always a reservoir of talent available—either ours or on other teams.

1439   In putting together a staff, I always wanted assistants who were, first, different from me and then different from each other.

1440   As a coach, when your team starts a streak going, you don't let up. Instead, you've got to be tough. You've got to be just the opposite of the way the players are. When your team wins two or three in a row, the players' friends tell them how great they are. But that's when you've got to pound that work ethic into them.

1441   California is really two different states, if not two different states of mind.

1442   You teach in meetings. You discuss on the practice field. You test in the game—*said when comparing coaching to teaching.*

1443   You'll be playing right here and that hole over there, that's where you'll be coming out of the tunnel from the locker room with 60,000 people cheering for you—*said, while assistant coach, to a newly recruited player during his first visit to San Diego State's Jack Murphy Stadium.*

1444   When one person controls everything, you get some people for and some against—and everyone is not together. But when everyone is equal, all ideas are treated equal.

1445   When you build collectively, what comes out is ours.

1446   When players collide with all that equipment on, it sounds like a car wreck.

1447   We believe every detail is important. It's the only way you can approach your job.

1448   So much of the game is spent feeling out the opponent, like a boxer spending five rounds seeing what the other guy can or can't do.

1449   The only yardstick for success our society has is being a champion. No one remembers anything else.

1450   Too many coaches want to be "one of the guys" but that's the worst thing a coach can be. Your players don't need another friend. Your players have all the friends they need. Sometimes too many. Your players need someone to tell them what to do. Your players need a coach, a teacher—not a friend.

1451   You have to tell the players what you want, you have to put it on a blackboard, you have to walk through it, you have to go through it at half-speed, then you have to run through it over and over until everybody's got it right.

1452   At one time or another each and every one of you is going to think about leaving here. Believe me, whether you're our first-round choice or the last free agent we signed, you'll think about going home. But when you start thinking about leaving, don't worry about it. Everybody thinks about it. Just remember that if you do leave and in another two or three years you want to come back, it'll be too late.

1453   You're going to get more publicity than you ever got in your life. Enjoy it—*said to his players before the Super Bowl XI.*

Johnny Majors

Coach: Iowa State 1968–1972, University of Pittsburgh 1973–1976, University of Tennessee 1977– . Record: 150-97-8.

1454   Coaches don't win football games. Players win games. Coaches don't go out there and line up.

1455   You're giving guys two or three of those fakes when you only need to give one. You're a great back. Fake once—once will be enough. Then cut yourself loose and run, run.

1456   I've always said that besides being good, you have to catch some breaks to win a national championship.

1457   I didn't want to bog them down with unrealistic curfews—*said when Pittsburgh went to New Orleans for the Sugar Bowl.*

1458   I've never had more fun in my life—*referring to Sugar Bowl victory.*

John F. "Chick" Meehan

Coach: Syracuse 1920–1924, New York University 1925–1931, Manhattan College 1932–1937. Record: 115-44-14.

1459   What's wrong with football? Nothing. It is still the greatest game in the world. No game can compare with it in preparing a boy for the competition of life. A football player must fight for everything he gets; nothing is handed to him. He struggles not so much to win recognition from his coach but from his fellows. Is there any better preparation than this for the still tougher battles ahead?

1460   I'll remove the butter from your systems—*reply when told his players ate too much butter.*

1461   We won't have the pressure of playing a big game every Sunday. That's why we'll get more fun out of the sport—*said when taking job at Manhattan College.*

1462   The boys were dressed in sweatshirts and sweatpants so that they could detrain at every stop and snap through light exercise and signal practice. Naturally we attracted small crowds. The team stopped about four times a day. From every town news dispatches were sent East saying that Syracuse had stopped off there for a brief workout—*referring to western trip in 1924 to play the University of Southern California.*

Harry Mehre

Coach: St. Thomas College 1922–1924, University of Georgia 1928–1937, University of Mississippi 1938–1945. Record: 98-60-7 (excludes St. Thomas).

1463   I really wasn't a very good recruiter. Oh, I went after the boys, all right, but I couldn't demean myself. I couldn't soft-soap a kid and his family to get him to sign when I knew I'd be chewing him out six months later.

1464   I would rather beat any team in the country than Yale. For to me and most of us, Yale means American football.

Leo R. "Dutch" Meyer

Coach: Texas Christian 1934–1952. Record: 109-79-13.

1465   They said I had my ends sitting in the stands spread out so wide they could sell soda water between plays.

1466   Fight them until hell freezes over, and then fight them on the ice.

Ronald S. "Ron" Meyer

Coach: University of Nevada 1973–1975, Southern Methodist University 1976–1981, New England Patriots 1982–1984, Indianapolis Colts 1986– . Record: 108-77-1.

1467   Playing defense today is like going into the boxing ring with one arm tied behind your back. It is really challenging.

1468   The professional game today is so flexible and so many things are thrown at you that we—the entire coaching staff—feel that nothing can be black and white. You have to adjust and adapt your own guidelines on the move.

1469   Once I had tasted the NFL, there was nothing that even compared to it. It was like flying a Cessna 172 compared to an F-16—*said when he left SMU to coach the New England Patriots.*

1470   The NFL has a singleness of purpose, and that's football and I like that.

Walter "Walt" Michaels

Coach: New York Jets 1977–1982, New Jersey Generals 1984–1985. Record: 66-62-1.

1471   Everyone feels fear. A man who has no fear belongs in a mental institution. Or on special teams.

1472   A 40-man squad with 15 real studs on it will be a winner. It's like a riot. Get three people yelling and pretty soon you've got 50, all chanting and hitting. Instigators—that's all it takes.

1473   You read a writer and many times you can see the other writers who had an effect on him when he was young. You can see something of them reflected in their work. It's the same in coaching.

1474   Your defensive game plan has no rhyme or reason if you can't try and project yourself into the other team's offense.

1475   I've never yet seen a dummy off the field that became a great thinker once he had the uniform on.

1476   Sometimes all a linebacker has to do is keep near his man. He may not even be called on to defend against a pass. What you want him to do is discourage a throw. Remember the quarterback only has a split second to look downfield and read the coverage, and if he sees a big linebacker near the back, that might be the only look he's going to have time for. He won't throw.

1477   When you blitz a lot you're also kidding yourself. Because the first thing a quarterback learns nowadays is how to read blitz coverage — and how to beat it. But hell, if we found a quarterback who couldn't read it, we'd blitz the hell out of him. You do what works for you.

1478   You can find people to play the defensive line — strong, dedicated, crazy people. But you have to have players to cover up for them. That's why linebackers were invented.

1479   It took me 20 years to learn what I've learned. Why should I just give it away? I don't speak at clinics and I don't write books on football.

1480   When the going gets tough, people usually revert to their traditional patterns. It's a psychological principle: you do best what you do most, and vice versa.

1481   You project yourself into the other coach's brain and determine what you would do if you were him. Then you try and counteract it.

1482   Don't forget a coach's first obligation is to his own college kids — not to you or to professional football. A lot of times you'll ask for prospects and he'll mention a marginal player who's just been a good, solid citizen for him for four years. He figures he might be able to get the kid a little bonus money. Who can blame him?

Clarence L. "Biggie" Munn

Coach: Albright College 1935–1936, Syracuse University 1946, Michigan State 1947–1953. Record: 152-35.

1483   Football today is a game of chess at high speed.

A. Earle "Greasy" Neale

Coach: Muskingum 1915, West Virginia Wesleyan 1916–1917, Marietta 1919–1920, Washington and Jefferson 1921–1922, University of Virginia 1923–1928, University of West Virginia 1931–1933, Philadelphia Eagles 1941–1950. Record: 141-98-16.

1484   The time to start worrying is when you don't hear from me. I pick on you because I care — *said to a player he constantly berated.*

1485   Figure the percentages. Always figure the percentages.

1486   You're never a quarterback until you reach the ten-yard line.

1487   With second and one, try for the long pass, the home run play. If you hit it, you're in gravy. If you don't you've still got two downs to go.

1488   If President Coolidge isn't in his seat at 2:00 P.M. he's going to miss some of the action, because we're not holding the kickoff for anyone—*said when Coolidge was to visit Virginia and Neale wanted game started on time.*

1489   I wrote 154 letters and still didn't get a job—*referring to his job search after leaving the University of West Virginia.*

1490   It said, "Your services are no longer required." That was the end of my coaching—*referring to a telegram.*

1491   We did everything but beat them.

1492   He is one of the most ferocious blockers and tacklers in the league who manages to use his shoulders, head, arms, hands, legs and sometimes even fingernails, all at the same time—*referring to center Alex Wojciechowicz, who joined Eagles in 1946.*

1493   Paul Brown should be a basketball coach. All he does is throw, throw and throw some more.

1494   Come Saturday night when you put your head on your pillow, say, "I've done everything I possibly could to prepare my team," and then go to sleep.

Robert R. Neyland

Coach: University of Tennessee 1926–1934, 1936–1940 and 1946–1952. Record: 173-31-12.

1495   The team that makes the fewest mistakes *wins.*

1496   Play for and make the breaks. When one comes your way *score.*

1497   If a break goes against you, don't let it get you down. Turn on *more* steam.

1498   Don't worry about it, Pat. We didn't come out here to tie them—*said to Pat Shires, who missed point after touchdown for Tennessee, giving the University of Texas a 14–13 lead. Tennessee went on to score one more touchdown and win.*

Charles H. "Chuck" Noll

Coach: Pittsburgh Steelers 1969– . Record: 193-140-1.

1499   It looked terrible in slow motion. But they don't play the game in slow motion—*said after seeing replay of Otis Wilson knocking out Louis Lipps.*

1500   If someone had told me before the game that we'd have 515 yards total offense and hold them to 171, I'd say we had a shoo-in. I think it shows the importance of getting the job done by special teams—*said to his team after losing to Kansas City Chiefs, 24–19.*

1501   Let's face it, if the Steelers were doing well, I wouldn't be here—*said a week after he joined club as coach.*

1502   No single assistant will be in charge of the overall defense or offense. The overall operation of the team is my responsibility.

1503   We did have one advantage—drafting fourth. But I don't want that advantage again.

1504   He doesn't go around people, he goes through people—*referring to Mean Joe Greene.*

1505   I'd like to see those guys thrown out of the league. They put a guy's whole career in jeopardy—*said of those who deliberately try to injure or maim others.*

1506   You, as a player, respect your quarterback more when the game's called on the field. But that's no small task. It takes a lot of preparation before he can do that. It's a lot easier calling the plays from the sidelines.

1507   A life of frustration is inevitable for any coach whose main enjoyment is winning.

1508   The nice thing about football is that you have a scoreboard to show you how you've done. In other things in life, you don't. At least not one you can see.

1509   There is one truism in this sport—you never arrive and you never can be satisfied.

1510   I just happen to believe a quarterback should run his own game and be given help only when he needs it.

1511   A good pitcher can completely dominate a game. A good quarterback still has to depend on the line in front of him, his backs and the men he throws to—*referring to a misconstrued comparison between a pitcher and quarterback.*

1512   I don't want a team whose players are more afraid of the coach than they are of their opponents.

1513   We have freedom of speech on the Steelers. All I ever tell my players is that they might have to suffer the consequences for what they say.

1514   The objective of football is not to break men's bodies and spirits; it's to win football games.

1515   The thrill isn't in the winning, it's in the doing.

1516   Winning is like a tightrope act. If you look down you get dizzy and you can fall. If you look straight ahead, always towards an objective you must reach, you keep going.

1517   I'm a teacher and the most important thing is teaching my students.

1518   All we can do out here is to provide a learning situation.

1519   If I'm making a spiel and I'm saying, "This is the way it is," and you as a prospective customer have an objection, I want to hear it. I really can't convince you about something unless I know the objection you have—*referring to his days as an insurance salesman.*

1520   The best way you can come down hard on them is by shipping them out—*referring to poor performers.*

1521   Discipline means no guessing.

1522   It's not the customary thing to run around and smack into other people. Not everybody wants to do it.

1523   People wonder why I look at them so long. Every time I go over them I can see a new thing—*referring to films of football games.*

1524   A local sportswriter called me and said, "You've been drafted. What's your reaction?" I thought he meant into the Army because the

Korean War was in progress then—*referring to the fact that he was drafted to play for the Cleveland Browns in 1953.*

1525   Someplace along your life you are going to have to function in a pressure situation and if you can learn to do it in a game where the results are not life and death, you can come to a situation where it is life and death and be better able to cope.

1526   Some good things came of that season—the players we drafted—*referring to the 1969 season, when Steelers were 1 and 13.*

1527   We'd better be. I couldn't take another season like this one—*reply to question about whether team would be improved after poor 1988 season.*

1528   Seems like suitable surroundings—*referring to the men's room, where he met sportswriters after losing a game.*

1529   It's a quick drop from the penthouse to the shithouse.

1530   If getting it wrong is necessary to eventually getting it right, well, we've done that part perfectly.

1531   The rewards of teaching or coaching are pretty much the same.

1532   Pride is at stake—*referring to a comment that the Steelers played well during a game in which nothing was at stake.*

1533   It is hard for a person from the outside to know what's going on on a team.

1534   I'm not going into combat. The players are.

1535   We'll take those little crumbs—*referring to this game-winning play: Pittsburgh losing to Oakland, 7–6, with less than a minute to go—Pittsburgh's Terry Bradshaw throws a pass—an Oakland player deflects the ball—the ball goes backwards about seven yards—Pittsburgh's Franco Harris catches it just before it hits the ground—he runs 42 yards for a touchdown.*

1536   We're putting the play in tomorrow—*referring to the same play.*

1537   People don't sell things for social reasons.

1538   Government's getting too big. It's like a mycelium.

1539   If you are doing it right, you don't get hit in the head. You hit the other guy.

1540   Come in low and strike a rising blow.

1541   There are some people who are not going to be up to the challenge. But that doesn't mean the challenge is wrong.

1542   Today and the future are all that count.

1543   There's only one way to coast and that's downhill.

1544   She says she's just finished doing the laundry and is in the middle of ironing and still has the cleaning to do. Well, that's the way it is with the coaches—*relating his wife's never ending series of chores with his.*

1545   Most teams are reluctant to trade quality players. If they have one up for trade, it's because he may be unhappy in his situation. You must measure that—whether you can satisfy him or help him with his problem.

1546   Originally I felt pro football was a part-time career, a stepping-stone after graduating from college to what you would do in your life.

1547   You start copying someone and you wind up doing a second-rate job because that's what a copy is—a second-rate imitation.

1548   If I'd had a third leg, I would have kicked myself—*said after making a mistake.*

1549   You never relax, never rejoice very long.

1550   I became aware of how much I wasn't aware of as a player—*said after he went from player to assistant coach.*

1551   A teacher, or coach, cannot wander because he works with attention spans that are short for what he must accomplish.

1552   If I wasn't able to go in and change something, then I didn't want it.

1553   People who achieve, concentrate.

Frank J. "Buck" O'Neill

Coach: Colgate 1902 and 1904–1905, Syracuse 1906–1907, 1913–1915 and 1917–1919, Columbia 1920–1922. Record: 81-41-8.

1554   When I get down on my Irish knees tonight to thank God for many favors, I will ask Him to bless each one of you gathered here today—*said during halftime ceremony during game at Syracuse honoring his election to the College Football Hall of Fame.*

Benjamin G. "Bennie" Oosterban

Coach: University of Michigan 1948–1958. Record: 63-33-4.

1555   "My fault" never has won a contest. Neither has "I'm sorry."

1556   Last Saturday's efforts won't win this Saturday's contest.

1557   Only a fool underestimates his opponent.

1558   Victory is sweat.

1559   The next effort is the important one.

1560   Be positive. The place for doubt is in the dictionary.

Thomas W. "Tom" Osborne

Coach: University of Nebraska 1973– . Record: 168-38-2.

1561   In some places football tickets might be one of the first things to go. But with a lot of people in Nebraska, the football tickets would be one of the last things to go. You can do without a lot of other things before you give up football tickets, because you know you may not get another shot at them. People have made a lot of sacrifices to have enough money to see the games and stay overnight — *referring to the passion for football versus the economic hardships in agricultural and ranching communities.*

1562   They may not be stars. Maybe he didn't play a lot. But a guy who could come down here and play and letter is of some importance to that community — *said of players from small Nebraska towns.*

1563   He's the only guy I know who wears his whole bank account around his neck — *referring to a player who wore several gold chains.*

Stephen J. "Steve" Owen

Coach: New York Giants 1931–1953, Toronto Argonauts (CFL) 1959, Calgary Stampeders (CFL) 1960, Saskatchewan Roughriders (CFL) 1961–1962, Syracuse Stormers (UFL) 1963. Record: 174-139-20 (excludes Syracuse).

1564   What do you think about just coming down to New York City on Sundays? You could stay in condition up there and just come for the games—*said during World War II, when Owen was desperate for men, to Mel Hein, football coach at Union College in Schenectady. Hein played three years as a "Sunday center," commuting back and forth to Schenectady.*

1565   Football is a game played down in the dirt and always will be.

1566   Football was invented by a mean son of a bitch and that's the way the game's supposed to be played.

1567   Shoot him before he leaves the dressing room—*referring to how to defend against Bronko Nagurski.*

1568   A little boy can carry a football because it's real light—*said to convince a player to switch from playing offense to defense.*

Duane C. "Bill" Parcells

Coach: Air Force 1978, New York Giants 1983– . Record: 72-57-1.

1569   It's the beauty of sports. The other team can be better, but you can be better that day.

1570   He's been in there with the chicken and the sheep, now he's got to go out there with the timberwolves—*referring to Karl Nelson, who was out in '87 with Hodgkin's disease, had major surgery on his left shoulder in January '88, and was put in starting lineup at start of next season.*

1571   You hit your own lotto—*said to Eric Schubert who kicked five field goals of 24, 36, 24, 41 and 33 yards in game against Tampa Bay Buccaneers. Giants won, 22–20.*

1572   I think life's too short to walk around with your teeth gritted all the time. I like to joke. I like to laugh.

1573   There ought to be a school someplace coaches could go to.

1574   I have one big expression, one big theme, when it comes to sports: Winning is never final.

1575   The game isn't 50 minutes.

1576   To heck with a first down. Let's go deep. I want it all.

1577   Some players come from smaller colleges where they didn't receive the proper coaching or face strong competition. A coach has to determine whether that player's potential is worthwhile even though there may be an absence of technique when compared with someone from a major college. You have a philosophy about each position and you have to ask yourself: Does that player fit the mold?

1578   I work horrible hours as a coach, but at least Judy Parcells knows where her husband is.

1579   It is shit work, no matter how wonderful the head coach is, and the relationship you have with the other assistants—*referring to being an assistant coach.*

1580   When the time comes that they want to get rid of you, a contract is a dishrag.

1581   You've got to be careful not to confuse sacks with hits. Just because a guy is sacked five times doesn't mean he's been hit hard five times.

1582   I've never met a guy that tough. You could do anything to him—drop him from a building, from an airplane, anything—and he'll show up to play. He's one of my parking lot guys, the kind who would just nod their heads, pack their bags and be early if I told them we had a game in some shopping center parking lot, for no money, at 6:00 A.M. some Wednesday. He just loves it—*referring to Jim Burt.*

1583   We had 78 good snaps and a bad one—*said after Phil Simms fumbled snap from center, Dallas recovered and kicked field goal to beat Giants.*

1584   God gives it to you and God takes it away.

1585   What happened out there?—*asked after team was shut out in '85 divisional playoffs.*

1586   We buried all the ghosts—*said after team won '86 Super Bowl.*

1587   I rant and rave after we win. I tell them, "Don't believe what the newspapers say about how good you are." Then, when the reporters are telling them they're bad, I'm telling them the opposite. I think it's my job to keep it in the proper perspective.

1588   Football coaches know a lot about selling: themselves, their program, their philosophy, their offense and defense.

1589   You get more than one chance with me.

1590   You can't just get 'em back and plug 'em in like light bulbs, fellas—*referring to Carl Banks, who in 1988 spent preseason in contract negotiations, didn't practice that much or put his heart in it and whom other teams beat on defense because he wasn't in top form.*

1591   It's part beauty pageant and part game show, the NFL draft.

1592   If you're not on top, you're nothing in this world.

1593   We're going to have a better team out there this year or there isn't going to be anybody left standing, including me.

1594   Winning is all that counts. The important thing is, find a way to win.

1595   This is private enterprise. The fans are entitled to the best product I can put on the field every Sunday, week in and week out, year in and year out if I'm lucky. How I put that product out there is my damn business.

1596   Testing is the only way to save lives and careers—*referring to the drug problem in football.*

1597   I've always tended to be very respectful of the guys that have come before me in this business.

1598   We've lost a couple of close games we could have won, and won a couple of close games we could have lost.

1599   War, that's what it'll be like.

1600   You can only really yell at the players you trust.

1601   Don't worry about it. It's just a bunch of guys with an odd-shaped ball.

Raymond K. "Buddy" Parker

Coach: Chicago Cardinals 1949, Detroit Lions 1951–1956, Pittsburgh Steelers 1957–1964. Record: 104-75-9.

1602   I'm through with this team. I'm getting out. This is the worst team I've ever seen—I've seen enough in training camp—and I like winning too much to go through a losing season—*said at a Lions preseason banquet, after which, Parker stalked out and quit.*

1603   I just said what I thought and that's it.

1604   I can't handle this team. It's the worst team I've ever seen in training camp. I don't mean material-wise. We've got good boys, but there has been no life ... no go ... it's a completely dead team.

1605   I don't want to get in the middle of another losing season. I think somebody else could handle it better.

1606   I had noticed how so many teams let down the two minutes before the half and the last two minutes of a game. It seemed you could get things done then that you couldn't do in the other 56 minutes of play. So we drilled on it—every day.

1607   You only lost a game. I could have lost my job—*said to the losing coach after his Lions had gotten off to a bad start at the beginning of the season, then won a game.*

1608   The trouble with most coaches is that they want to make the game too damn complicated.

1609   I didn't want to tell them what not to do. I wanted to stress what they had to do, and that was win.

1610   If you've got to ride herd on players, then you've got the wrong kind of players and you won't win with them.

1611   I wasn't building for the future—I had to win right then—*referring to the reason for trading away draft choices.*

Ara R. Parseghian

Coach: University of Miami (OH) 1951–1955, Northwestern 1956–1963, Notre Dame 1964–1974. Record: 170-58-6.

1612   We may very well be the last bastion of discipline left in the United States. The military doesn't have it the way it used to; schools, churches and families don't have it. Athletics might be the only thing left where a young man, for two hours or so a day, yields himself to us because he wants to be part of a team.

1613   The game is not won by a pep talk on Saturday. It's won by preparation of your club from Monday until game time.

1614   One reckless pass and it could have cost us the game. I wasn't going to do a jackass thing like throw it away at the last minute—*said after Notre Dame came from behind to tie a game in the closing minutes, regained the ball on its own thirty, then stayed on the ground instead of going for the long "bomb" and a possible touchdown.*

1615   The moments of splendor, the ruthlessness of injury, the private inner sanctum of one's naked feeling exposed in loss or victory, the humor and tragedy of men at play and work can never be captured totally in words or pictures.

1616   Give me a reason I can hang my hat on and I'll accept any logical suggestion.

1617   I'm sure your mother would rather look at your back on the bench than see you carried off the field on a stretcher. You're not ready to play and I'm not going to risk it.

1618   When I make a fist it's strong and you can't tear it apart. As long as there's unity, there's strength. We must become so close with the bonds of loyalty and sacrifice, so deep with the conviction of sole purpose, that no one, no group, no thing, can ever tear us apart. If your loyalty begins to fade it becomes easier to go out and have a beer, to slack off a little in practice, to go listen to those who tell you you should be playing ahead of someone else. If that happens, this fist becomes a limp hand.

1619   There ought to be a way to penalize officials, too.

1620   Two weeks after Navy I told the team they were definitely causing my hair to turn gray. Today I told them they were going to make me a replacement for Kojak.

1621   Everything worthwhile must be bought with sacrifice.

1622   The great teams, because of pride, coaching and loyalty, are never broken, even in losing efforts.

1623   There are thousands of things we could say. There are officials and the calls we could blame. But when we won this year, we won as Notre Dame men—fair, hard and with humility. To be less than that at this moment, to cry foul, to alibi, would undo much that this season has done. For the next ten minutes no one will be allowed in here. If you've got to scream, if you want to cry, swear or punch a locker, do it now. I can understand all those sentiments. But after we open the doors I want all of you to hold your tongues, to lift your heads high and in the face of defeat be Notre Dame men—*said after loss to Southern California in 1964.*

1624   I prefer to think of our record as 9¾ to ¼, not 9 and 1—*said after winning first nine games of the '64 season, then losing the next after having the lead most of the game.*

1625   There's no other way than repeating it over and over again.

1626   Your problem is that you're like a sponge. When water hits you, you absorb it, get heavy and eventually sink. When water hits a duck, it rolls right off his back and he stays buoyant.

1627   Success won't happen by sitting here. We've got to keep on striving. We've got to recruit, explore new ideas, improve old techniques and know, really know our players.

1628 No one hates seeing a player hurt more than I. It is the stinking part of the game no one can control. But whatever you feel, play clean. The worst thing you can do to any team is beat them. Let's do it hard and clean with class.

1629 There's no game more important that the one you're playing today.

1630 Take the personnel, see what they can do best, and let them dictate strategy. Don't start with strategy first.

1631 Football coaching is an unstable business.

1632 I think when a team is as emotionally high as we were it is better to begin the game on defense. If an error occurs due to over-anxiousness, your chances of being hurt seriously aren't as great.

1633 You just once get flat, you just once relax and someone will fatten up their reputation at your expense.

1634 You gave your best and you must concede something to worthy opponents.

1635 These unique team experiences are part of the lure of athletics for all those who choose to make it such a major part of their lives. We already accept that the interest and adrenalin, the tears and the grief, are not just restricted to the players; thousands of spectators cheer and despair, follow and report, on behalf of 'their team.' It is an identity, a link, something to get excited about and pull for, that adds purpose to their lives.

1636 It's easy to be loyal when you're winning. The real test of attitude is when things turn sour.

1637 Quarterbacks and head coaches get too much credit and too much blame.

1638 My doctor didn't order me to quit. But I found myself taking blood pressure pills, tranquilizers and sleeping pills and that's not right. So I backed off and said, "What the hell is happening?" It's not a 12-month job; it's more than that. You can't understand the demands of this job until you walk in the shoes of the man who has it.

1639 This will be the last time I walk out of this locker room at halftime and I want this win. I want it for Notre Dame.

Joseph V. "Joe" Paterno

Coach: Penn State 1966– . Record: 220-57-3.

1640   I consider football merely as just another extracurricular activity like debating, the band or anything else on campus.

1641   If coaches are to have any stability and security, they need to be treated like an English professor.

1642   I consider myself an educator in charge of an area of responsibility in the university, just as the head of the English or History Department.

1643   At Penn State, coaches are given faculty rank and they are considered to be educators. I am a full professor and two of my assistant coaches are associate professors.

1644   He was on his way to Princeton and got lost—*referring to how he recruited a player.*

1645   I firmly believe that no coach should have less than a four-year contract when he takes a job at a new school. The first year he's working with his predecessor's material and that's not a fair test. The second year, his recruits are sophomores and still learning. The third year is when he should find out whether or not he can do the job. The fourth year is the real test, and if he can't win then, he should move on.

1646   Some days I feel like I've got a hundred sons to worry about.

1647   You'd better start looking for another coach because I'm getting out of here. I'll go nuts in this town—*said to Penn State's head coach in 1950, soon after Paterno began working there as one of his assistants.*

1648   To me, the word "competition" is related to the word "compassion." The more you pit yourself against the other guy and he pits himself against you, the better you understand each other because you're both struggling for the same thing in the same way.

1649   We try to remember football is part of life and not life itself.

1650   I'm against it. I'm against anything that people can hang things from—*referring to a dome for Penn State's stadium.*

1651   The players who have been most important to the success of Penn State teams have just naturally kept their priorities straight: football a high second, but academics an undisputed first.

1652   Everything costs. No accomplishment comes without suffering. *Humanum est pati.*

1653   Kick the ball deep into the opponent's territory and scrap like hell to keep it there.

1654   I don't care if my players like me. I want them to like me when it's important they like me, when they're out in the world, raising families, using their degrees. I want them to like me when it hits them what I've been trying to say all these years.

1655   A dazzling, great passing quarterback lives in an environment that is the essence of vulnerability. His job description requires that he part with the ball.

1656   Football games are won or lost on five or six plays. The trouble is you never know when they're coming.

1657   The minute you think you've got it made, disaster is just around the corner.

1658   The game belongs to whoever decides to take it.

1659   Winning isn't everything. I'll never buy that thing that if a boy loses a football game he's a loser for life.

1660   Bud Wilkenson once told me that if a single one of his coaches mentioned that practice was getting too long, he would cut it down. That's generally a good rule.

1661   Screaming doesn't do anything. Reality tells a lot more.

1662   Coaching isn't a popularity contest.

1663   Why is it necessary, if a team wins by a point, to make them heroes and the other guys bums? I'd like to see us watch the game for the sheer excitement of it—the pageantry, the beauty, the great competition going on down there on the field.

1664   We had lost our victory—but not our excellence or worth.

1665   The epic is not about the victory, but about the glorious struggle.

1666   A lot of bowl people think a playoff would detract from the bowls. Not me. A playoff would add more meaning to the games.

1667   So in a couple of years, maybe we'd have gone to the Super Bowl. So what? Here I have the opportunity to affect the lives of a lot of young people—and not just on my football team. I'm not kidding myself that that would be true at the professional level—*said when he turned down opportunity to coach New England Patriots in '73 to stay with Penn State.*

1668   My swing—*reply when asked what his handicap was in golf.*

1669   The best teacher is not only the person who has the most knowledge, but the one who has his knowledge best organized and who knows how to state what he knows in different ways.

1670   A coach's first duty is to coach minds.

1671   If coaches have to teach kids, older coaches have to teach kid coaches.

1672   Our object in playing hard is not violence but what we call attrition—hitting the guy, hitting the guy, hitting the guy, until he gets tired of getting hit.

1673   Women's sports have arrived. They give women another way of feeling good about themselves.

1674   There isn't any problem that can't be solved when the players involved and the coach sit down and consult about it. The trouble is, at some places third parties get involved in something they don't really know anything about, and it's no longer a player-coach relationship.

1675   Better make mine bulletproof—*referring to waterproof jackets ordered for the team.*

1676   Every game symbolizes the tragedy—the cost of every victory is that sombody's got to lose.

1677   Coaches of pro teams eventually lose their players to smashed knees, crushed discs, aging and arthritis. College coaches lose them to the bittersweet of graduation.

1678   Most of today's NCAA rules on recruiting are useless handcuffing, downright stupid and just about beg some coaches to cheat.

1679   There's an oddity about college football not generally shared by any other sport: it brings more fame and prestige to a guy who doesn't play— the coach—than it does to anyone who imperils his bones on the field.

1680   A football coach is at the pivot of a big business.

Ray Perkins

Coach: New York Giants 1979–1982, University of Alabama 1983–1986, Tampa Bay Buccaneers 1987– . Record: 70-83-1.

1681   When you bring a player to campus to recruit him, the last thing he wants to see is the stadium. He's only going to spend a few hours there every year. He wants to see the athletic dormitories, the weight room, the locker room. He's going to be living in those places, not the stadium.

1682   I don't know. I don't see her that much—*reply when asked what his wife's reaction was to his long working hours.*

1683   The plays come from the press box and the field. The bad plays come from the box and good plays come from the field.

1684   In my system, if you want to play then you've got to practice.

1685   To me, being a success is doing what I want to do. It's not measured by how much money I make.

O. A. "Bum" Phillips

Coach: Texas Western 1962, Houston Oilers 1975–1980, New Orleans Saints 1981–1985. Record: 90-85-1.

1686   Coaches are very important. Hell, you can get the players off the back of a Wheaties box.

1687   There are two types of coaches. Them that have just been fired and them that are going to be fired.

1688   The only time I want anyone mad around me is on Sunday afternoon and then we all can be mad together at the guys in the other jerseys.

1689   If I have to tell a guy "Do it" because I'm the head coach, then there is a little bit of doubt whether or not I am.

1690   Two kinds of football players ain't worth a damn. The one that never does what he's told and the other that never does anything except what he's told.

1691   Flu doesn't keep you from playing football. It just makes you uncomfortable. If you're sick, you can always call time-out, throw up and keep on playing.

1692   He can take his'n and beat your'n or he can take your'n and beat his'n—*referring to Don Shula.*

1693   It was like cutting my own boy, but he took it a lot better than I did. He consoled me—*referring to firing Mike Simpson, whom Phillips had coached in both high school and while an assistant at the University of Houston, from the Oilers.*

1694   A school superintendent I once worked for told me, "Don't ever force a guy to tell you, 'No.' If it's real important to you and you can see you might get a 'No,' don't force the issue. Walk away."

1695   Anything that would happen, he would say, "My fault." Regardless of what happened, he never was one who would blame another person. The coaches and players who kept hearing that after awhile began to think, "Well, it wasn't all your fault. I could have done something better." That was his method of getting more out of people. He was a master at it—*referring to Bear Bryant.*

1696   When you start out in high school, you must take whoever is out there and play with them.

1697   You teach there by explaining something over and over—*referring to high school coaching.*

1698   I went in as a private and 31 months later I came out as a private. The Marine Corps was real spit and polish. I wasn't.

1699   If I drop dead tomorrow, at least I'll know I died in good health.

1700   My idea of discipline is not making guys do something, it's getting them to do it. There's a difference between bitching and coaching.

1701   We knocked on the door this time. Next year we'll knock it down.

1702   Time is one of the two things you fight in football—time and the scoreboard.

1703   The good teams don't change a lot.

1704   It's not what you can do; it's what you can get those players to do.

1705   There are a multitude of offensive sets but you can't run all of them. You must narrow them down to what you can do best and what fits your people the best. The quickest way to learn that is coaching in high school.

1706   You work to strengthen your weakest link, not worry about the strongest one.

1707   If the assistant coach is telling them what I want told, I don't care whether they think I thought of it as long as they do it.

1708   Show me an emotional coach on the sidelines and I'll show you a team that will mirror everything he does.

1709   The film looks suspiciously like the game itself—*said after seeing film of game he lost by wide margin.*

1710   I think the player deserves the right to be told by the head coach—*referring to cutting athletes from the team.*

1711   When you have to cut a player, it's not necessarily that he can't play, it's just that he may not be able to play for you.

1712   If they like me, they're going to respect me.

1713   I don't believe in threatening people because I don't like to get threatened.

1714   I'd rather have preparation than motivation.

1715   Everyone likes to play and no one likes to practice.

1716   When you think it's your system that's winning, you're in for a damn big surprise.

1717   I take my wife with me everywhere because she is too ugly to kiss good-bye.

1718   I teach them to get along with their fellow man—the other players. If you don't teach that in coaching, then you're not coaching.

1719   I know I said that this was just another game, but I lied—*said after Houston beat Dallas.*

1720   He didn't coach football, he coached people—*said of Bear Bryant.*

1721   I can sure tell them what not to do—*referring to guiding players and the knowledge gained from his own mistakes.*

1722   I thought I did until I looked at some old game films—*reply when asked if he ever played college football.*

1723   We're not giving away any football players who could hurt us later. I don't mind people thinking I'm stupid but I don't want to give them any proof.

1724   Everyone will forget you when you leave the game and all you will have left are the things it has taught you—to sacrifice, to work hard.

1725   People demand to see a winner and they deserve to do so. If you don't have one, somebody's got to suffer.

1726   There's a whole lot of things in the world more important than winning football games.

1727   I've always said the things I say now. But when I was coaching at Nederland High School, nobody came around to write them down.

Tommy Prothro

Coach: Oregon State 1955–1964, UCLA 1965–1970, Los Angeles Rams 1971–1972, San Diego Chargers 1974–1978. Record: 139-106-7.

1728   I prefer the language of the Olympics, in which you say somebody won second.

1729   The only way you can rebuild this team is to draft young players and play them. That means we're gonna lose. Believe me, it's going to be terrible but that's the only way these people can get the experience they need—*said after joining Chargers.*

1730   If each of you goes out there and plays the best game you'll ever play, if each of you plays over his head, and if each of them plays the worst game they'll every play, the worst game of their lives, we still don't have a chance—*said before first game of '75 season.*

1731   I knew we were going to lose, but I didn't know we were going to lose this much—*said after Chargers lost their first 11 games in 1975.*

1732   We've just got to have patience.

1733   If I have an ability in coaching it's teaching, not strategy.

1734   I really don't learn by reading things. I learn by seeing something and talking about it.

1735   You never know when they are going to do something, but if you know something they won't do, then you don't have to protect against it.

John Ralston

Coach: Utah State 1959–1962, Stanford 1963–1971, Denver Broncos 1972–1976. Record: 119-80-7.

1736   Football isn't all a game of plans and finesse. Down on the field it can be as physical as a street fight.

1737   My slogan is, "See yourself successful."

1738   When I started out coaching in high school, I tried to do everything. I tried to direct the offensive and defensive units, the kicking units—to carry the whole burden. When I moved up to the college level I continued to do this for a number of years, but then I gradually realized you couldn't. I began to delegate more and more duties, to leave myself free to worry about only four main considerations: (1) to decide what we'll do in all kicking situations; (2) to keep track of the combinations of scores, so that I know, for example, when it might be unwise to settle for a field goal; (3) to note certain changes we should make in our offensive and defensive strategies at halftime; and (4) to act as a sort of cheerleader, to keep the individual players up. I guess that's probably the most important thing I do.

1739   I left because of illness and fatigue. The fans were sick and tired of me.

1740   You either grow up or you go.

1741   The problems of industry are no different than those of a football coach.

1742   The big thing when I came to the NFL—and it hasn't changed—is communication. Young people want to know why.

1743   Hell, football is an emotional business and I'll go home and I'll cry to get it out of my system.

1744   New people coming in, older ones moving out is the nature of the business. But the longer the older hands stay with you, the better it is because they help pass on your philosophy.

1745   The highs and lows of coaching are monumental.

1746   Nothing is more fun than winning.

1747   College teams run about 90 plays a game while pro teams run anywhere from 45 to 70.

1748   It's perpetual motion for six seconds.

1749   A team has to feel like a team. It has got to believe that it has been better prepared for each game than the other team. It's up to the coach to provide this preparation and to supply the motivation that gets his players ready to produce at top performance. Every coach goes about that a different way. Basically what he is after is attitude — attitude — a-t-t-i-t-u-d-e. That's the magic word.

1750   Good football has changed. When I was a player, you could tell a boy to run through a brick wall and he would. Today you're coaching individuals and you don't coach an athlete, you coach a mind.

1751   The tyrannical coach often is controlled by his own demands of ego and emotion.

1752   The tough part of college coaching is relating to young people, not the recruiting, which is nothing more than getting on that road and staying there.

1753   They want to have a creative input into the overall picture — *referring to the modern day athlete.*

1754   To play this game you must be smart — not smart aleck. There is a tremendous difference between these two.

1755   The belief that doing it till it is right is nothing more than the belief that excellence doesn't come easy.

Daniel E. "Dan" Reeves

Coach: Denver Broncos 1981– . Record: 78-49-1.

1756   I daily ask the Lord for wisdom.

1757   To me, the biggest fallacy is in the people's perception of Christianity and their belief that you can't be a Christian and still be competitive.

1758   When you read the Bible, you'll find many places where it definitely says you don't have to live your life without being competitive. It says, for instance, in Paul that "The race is to the swift."

1759   We all have an opportunity to touch people's lives. I'm glad that I have it in a positive way.

1760   The one thing I've discovered as a head coach is that every time

I think, "Nothing new can possibly happen, nothing new can come up next year I haven't already dealt with," something does.

1761   Nothing stays the same.

1762   Games are won and lost on minute things.

1763   This game is so fleeting.

1764   It was my first year as a coach and I thought, "Boy, this is an easy business."

1765   It makes no difference what you are in, you are going to have problems.

1766   You don't like them but you have to live with them. And they happen every year—*referring to meetings where he tells players they're cut from the team.*

1767   You hear from people you haven't heard from since high school—*referring to people asking for tickets for sold-out games.*

1768   It's easy for people to get along, to have companionship and as you hear said so many times in sports, live for one another, when they are winning. The true test is when you are losing.

1769   The toughest thing to do in this business is be a backup quarterback.

1770   You're never out of a game with Elway as quarterback—*referring to John Elway.*

1771   This game, if you don't have some fun out of it, if you don't relax, forget about things, go out to have some fun, this game is miserable.

1772   The guy that gets fired is the coach, not the general manager.

1773   You think of the Rose Bowl as the epitome of college and professional football—this huge famous stadium—but the dressing rooms are archaic. There is no room.

1774   Dana was born on Tuesday and I didn't get to see her until the following Monday. I do think that you have to be a special kind of woman to be a wife of a professional football coach.

1775   He had an owner that allowed him time to get the job done. And he had the power to get the job done—*referring to Coach Tom Landry and owner Clint Murchison.*

1776   Little bitty things make the big difference.

1777   A successful team, a star player, a coach, we all have to know it isn't going to last forever.

1778   Drinking is the macho thing to do and that's an image that has betrayed people from the time they are in high school.

1779   It's a drug you do with people. And if you've got money, then those people are definitely going to want to be around you because you are the one that is going to supply the cocaine.

1780   I'm not saying all three hundred pounders are steroid products. But some are.

1781   Testing is a great deterrent. If a person has a problem, testing will help that person keep clean.

1782   You are functioning without intestines—*referring to losing.*

1783   Remember this. Remember how much it hurts—*said to players after losing Super Bowl.*

1784   We were good enough to get there. We were not good enough to win. And all people will remember is the second part, not the first—*referring to losing Super Bowl.*

1785   I have a sign on my office wall, right across from my desk. It says, "Difficulties in life are intended to make us better, not bitter."

1786   Adversity molds people's lives more than success.

1787   There is no question in my mind that I am where I am right now because this is where the Lord wants me.

Edward G. "Eddie" Robinson

Coach: Grambling 1941–1942 and 1945– . Record: 358-125-15.

1788   They changed the name of the school to Grambling University. Used to be when the other team was down at our goal line, our students would yell, "Hold that line, Louisiana Negro Normal and Industrial Institute!" Before they could finish the cheer, the other guys would score.

1789   Leadership, like coaching, is fighting for the hearts and souls of men, to get them to believe in you.

1790   I like to see my players come to me as boys and leave as men.

1791   I really believe "my country 'tis of thee."

1792   I learned very early on that despite a lot of obstacles, America gives you opportunity. And maybe that's the most important thing I can impress on my players.

1793   I try and tell the kids what's out there when football is done with and they have to compete in life. I let them know quickly that there must be agreement between verb and subject.

1794   The kids cried, but in their hearts I know they understood me and were with me—*said after team lost 9–7 on final play, from one-foot line, going for touchdown instead of field goal.*

1795   Balance is our key and intensive practice provides our sharpness.

1796   Money is no big deal. I've never had a contract here. What I value most is my family and what I got from my mama and daddy.

1797   Blacks must get out and compete. When they leave here and go into pro ball, I don't want them to come back and say they didn't make it because they're black. If the white boy beats you fairly, be sure you understand he beat you because he was better, not because you're black.

1798   I still want to coach a boy as if he were my own son.

1799   I'm old-fashioned. To me there's still a right way and there's a wrong way.

1800   I don't mind you falling asleep, but do you have to do it against my shoulder—*said to a player watching films of game.*

1801   They should believe in the Deity—*he made church service at New Rocky Valley Southern Baptist Church "required" by distributing the laundry allowance there.*

1802   If you think you have two strikes on you because you're black and you aren't allowed to do anything, then you'll strike out.

1803   They're not going to relay their message through me—*referring to black militants.*

1804   If a man doesn't stand up for what he believes in, he's not worth a damn.

1805   You know, when they call the roll, I would like to feel I have made some positive contribution to society, some little something. Coaching for coaching's sake is fine, but there are other things—like teaching boys to compete in society—and I don't know if I could have done some things I've done anywhere else than Grambling.

John A. Robinson

Coach: University of Southern California 1976–1982, Los Angeles Rams 1983– . Record: 138-64-2.

1806   We should have put a ribbon on the football. We were handing them gifts all day.

1807   In professional football you're always going to have contract squabbles. Players who want a better contract. Players who don't sign when they're drafted. Players who want to renegotiate their contracts. That's part of the business. And as a coach you have to cope with that.

1808   3–0 in the NFL is 3–0 in the NFL—*said in response to criticism that first three teams Rams played in '88 season were weak and had a combined 2–7 won-lost record.*

1809   Problems with communication begin with the first day you start coaching.

1810   More motion, more camouflage, make it more difficult for the defense to zero in on the things we do.

1811   We're going to keep running and wear the other team down. Things that don't work in the first quarter will work in the fourth quarter because we've worn the other team down.

1812   He can run on grass. He can run on gravel if he has to. Or on a beach. Or in a wheatfield—*referring to Eric Dickerson of the Rams.*

1813   There wasn't a whole lot of scoring, just a bunch of guys on both sides fighting their butts off to win the football game. It may not be exciting to some folks who don't understand that part of football, but it was the kind of football I love.

Knute K. Rockne

Coach: Notre Dame 1918–1930. Record: 102-12-5.

1814   . . . and go out there and fight, fight, fight, fight . . .

1815   "Someday, Rock," he said, "when the team's up against it, when things are going wrong and the breaks are beating the boys, tell them to go in there with all they've got and win just one for the Gipper. I don't know where I'll be then, Rock, but I'll know about it and I'll be happy." All right, boys, let's go get them. This is the game!

1816   Now go out there and crucify them.

1817   The secret of coaching success can be reduced to a simple formula: strict discipline in your training program on the field combined with a high and continued interest in all your other relationships with your kids.

1818   If you go hunting with your boy, you won't have to go hunting for your boy.

1819   Fight to live! Fight to win! Fight to live! Fight to win-win-win!

1820   Play tough, play fair, play to win. Don't beef if you lose, but don't lose.

1821   Boys must have an outlet for animal spirits.

1822   There's too much of a mistaken idea about this character stuff.

1823   I don't know what you mean by that tired phrase "character building." But if you mean it was stopping boys from smoking, swearing or keeping late hours, I'm not your man.

1824   Take him out and buy him a few beers . . . but don't tell him it was my idea.

1825   Drink the first. Sip the second slowly. Skip the third.

1826   Football is a game played with the arms, legs and shoulders, but mostly from the neck up.

1827   Learn to live that ground. Keep those legs spread and grip that good earth for hard contact, both before and after contact.

1828   Use all your power in your hips and thighs. That's where nature placed it.

1829   Love to block and let them know you like it.

1830   I want you cocky at all times. At all times without letup—*advice to his quarterbacks.*

1831   I'll be glad to supply the two cents. Do you want to take it off right here or in the locker room?—*reply to humiliated player who said for two cents he'd turn in his uniform.*

1832   I'm saving him for the Junior Prom—*referring to player whose social life caused him to be late for practice.*

1833   Yeah, that guy doesn't know his own strength, or anything else.

1834   At times they caused me a certain amount of pain and exasperation, but mainly they brought me great joy.

1835   Just before the game I read several telegrams to the team, and then one to the effect that my little boy, Billy, had suddenly become very seriously ill. Quite ill, in fact, and the telegram from my wife stated that the only thing that seemed to be worrying him was whether or not Daddy's team would win. She added, as I read the imaginary telegram, that she felt that if the team won, it would be the best thing that could happen for poor little Billy. Needless to say the team went out keyed to a razor edge and their tackling was the talk of Alabama for days. In fact, Red Barrow fumbled seven times that day from the effects of just sheer wild crushing tackles. But I can never use any similar trick again. In fact, now, years afterward, whenever I meet one of the old team, his lips will break into a sardonic grin as he inquires, "Well, how is your boy, Billy?" This was the first and last time I have ever used this sort of psychology.

1836   So this is the so-called Fighting Irish. You look to me like a lot of peaceful sissies. Well, I have been here too long to stand for this kind of nonsense and I quit. I resign right now! Tom, take charge of the team. As far as I'm concerned I never want to see any of you again and in my mind your names will be mud....

1837   It was really a great comeback. However this is the first and last time I expect to do anything like this, as I receive many a gibe from the old boys who played in the game whenever I meet them. As I look back on it, however, it was a sweet game to win and perhaps in this exceptional instance the psychology was warranted—*referring to the game in which he gave the speech above (entry 1836).*

1838   I'm going to watch the rest of the game from up in the stands—*said to show his disgust with team losing at halftime. It fought back to win.*

1839   Playing with boys' emotions is a dangerous thing and the coach who does so must pay for it.

1840   I beg your pardon. I thought this was a Notre Dame team—*said after opening door to team's locker room after it had played a disappointing first half.*

1841   Remember, girls, let's not have any rough stuff out there—*said after a disappointing first half.*

1842   When that game is over tomorrow, and I know you'll do everything possible to hold down the score, I'd like to ask you fine young men of Troy to come over and congratulate my boys on a fine game. It will mean so much to them to have a firm handshake and a kind word from a team like yours—*said to Southern California team in 1930, the day before it was to play underdog Notre Dame. Notre Dame won, 27–0.*

1843   One oration a season is quite enough for any football squad. Action brings reaction, and if the coach talks too much, his words lose weight.

1844   They tell me that this Roper is a great orator. You fellows just lay on the floor and listen to him while I save my voice—*referring to Princeton coach, Bill Roper, and fact that flimsy door separated teams' dressing rooms.*

1845   At home we're the hosts and I never liked the idea of being embarrassed in front of so many of our friends. On the road we're somebody else's guests—and we play in a way that they're not going to forget we visited them.

1846   Courage means to be afraid to do something and still going ahead and doing it.

1847   Teaching cooperation is not always the easiest thing in the world to do, especially to a group of boys.

1848   I'd rather have 11 men who are willing to follow orders than the most brilliant collection of individual stars on earth.

1849   Success is based on what the team does, not on how you look.

1850   You can't take any more out of an organization than you put into it.

1851   My policy has always been to be firm rather than strict: to act rather than talk.

1852   Yards don't win games. It's scoring points that counts.

1853   A winner never quits and a quitter never wins.

1854   The world pities a loser but it loves a winner. Don't ever forget it—in any game you're in.

1855   There is no reward for the loser.

1856   There is room at the top only for the few who have the ability and imagination and the daring and the personality and the energy that make them stand out from among their fellow men. But there is success for any man in his own job if he does it as well as it can be done. As far as I am able to observe, the greatest satisfaction I can get on this earth is to do the particular job I am doing as well as it can be done, and I think that holds good for anyone.

1857   It probably sounds farfetched now but I see the day coming when most college teams will be going by air exclusively.

1858   Why don't you come and sit on the bench with me?—*said to Mae Miller, first girl to sit on bench with Notre Dame players—1922.*

1859   I'll find out what my best team is when I find out how many doctors and lawyers and good husbands and good citizens have come off of each and every one of my teams.

1860   One thing nobody can ever take away from you is your own integrity.

1861   So the first thing you're going to do is crack those books. After you get up on your studies, then it's fine to play football.

1862   And once in awhile toss a little bit of Law so you'll know if you're right or wrong; throw in some Accounting so you'll know how to add up two and two.

1863   Keep yourself in such perfect shape that you'll get the best out of your body at all times.

1864   I assume you're all in shape. After all, you've only been out of it a half-dozen years—*said while recruiting for an old-timers game.*

1865   They didn't realize it but these youngsters were making a powerful impression on me with their devotion, and when I saw all of them walking up to the communion rail, and realized the hours of sleep they'd sacrificed, I understood for the first time what a powerful ally their religion was to them in their work on the football field....

1866   You're being a little tight with the wax, aren't you, Father—*said at his baptism. Only one candle was lit, six others were not. Rockne was a convert to Catholicism.*

1867   If football is a good sport for the varsity player, why isn't it a good sport for the entire undergraduate body? Granted that it is, I want everybody at Notre Dame who cares to kick a football to have someplace in which to kick it—*said after Notre Dame began a league for men in different dormitories.*

1868   Win or lose, I'm running this team.

1869   It's my show. If I flop, let them pan me. If we're a hit, let them say anything they want.

1870   Everybody likes to be a Monday morning quarterback. It's so easy to call the plays a day or two later.

1871   Always think three plays ahead. Then you've got the jump on them.

1872   The limits are boundless if you believe in yourself and are willing to pay the price.

1873   A football coach must pay the price for victory—that price is work and perspiration.

1874   They can't score if we control the ball.

1875   The breaks came my way when I had sense enough to take them; and while that's an unromantic way of explaining a career, it has the advantage of being the truth.

1876   Football teaches a boy a sense of responsibility—responsibility as a representative of his college, responsibility to his teammates, responsibility in controlling his passions, fear, hatred, jealousy and rashness. Football brings out the best there is in everyone.

1877   Life is competition. Success in life goes only to the man who competes successfully.

1878   They learn how to cooperate in team play, and cooperation is the essense of big business.

1879   Unless you understand the problems of production, engineering, bookkeeping, service, advertising and all the departments which go to make up your organization, you cannot succeed. The failure of any one of them may cause your business to fail—*said to executives of Studebaker, the former car company.*

1880   Remember what plays are working and what plays aren't working—particularly the former.

1881   When the other side wants to give you something, go get it.

1882   One loss is good for the soul. Too many losses are not good for the coach.

1883   Baloney! I've got some pretty good players who are willing to listen to me and do as I tell them. Then, of course, maybe that's the miracle, in view of the demands I make on them—*referring to the press calling him "The Miracle Coach."*

1884   A team should never be coddled in regard to their ailments, but rather should be made to adopt a Spartan attitude.

1885   Don't do as I do, do as I say. . . . A doctor advising a diabetic to avoid sugar doesn't have to follow his own advice.

1886   This thing is closer to beating me than anything I've ever known in my life—*said when Rockne had phlebitis.*

1887   The doctors say I'm taking a big chance coming over here, but I don't care. I don't care what happens after today . . . but I didn't come here to see you lose.

1888   Never have I wanted to win a game as badly as I want this one. And you can deliver it to me. But only if you go out there and hit 'em, hit 'em, hit 'em like they've never been hit before, like you've never hit anyone before!

1889   The docs had told me I was a 90 percent new man—and I say to hell with the other 10 percent.

1890   I remember last September I received a letter from one alumnus which went somewhat as follows: "I am personally delighted to hear that you recovered your health, but my personal opinion is that if that blood clot had been in your head instead of your leg, you would never have been laid up."

1891   Thank you but don't ever hold news like that from me again. I'd pass up a football game for my son any day—*said to assistants who kept back news about his son who was rushed to the hospital.*

1892   I'd never give a snap of my fingers for anybody who isn't scared to death before his event—*said to pole vaulter.*

1893   I lost to a farmer boy who had the toughest thumb in the country—*said when he lost in Notre Dame marbles tournament.*

1894   Mobility. Mobility and change of pace. That's what we need. They're not going to know where we're going or when we get there.

1895   Sure, but I'll not say it until they start giving baseball victories to the teams that have the most men left on base—*reply when asked if he was in agreement with a suggestion that a team get points for number of first downs and yards gained.*

1896   Perfection in petty details is most essential.

1897   When you're thinking about retaliation you are also forgetting what you are supposed to do, and who loses then? ... The next time somebody slugs you, walk away. Sure I know it's natural to want to punch back, but walk away. Show some discipline, some class. Turn it to your advantage. Remember, when the other guy is figuring out how he's going to get you again, he's not thinking about football.

1898   I tell them that I have no brief against playing pool long hours in the afternoon, dancing half the night or learning to drive a car with one hand, but I tell them that we have no time for it.

1899   If you spend the next three months practicing in the sand, you'll be that much faster when you report back here in the fall and resume playing on turf.

1900   Foul and dirty play is only an honest admission that your opponent is a better man than you.

1901   A team in an ordinary frame of mind will do only ordinary things. In the proper emotional stage, a team will do extraordinary things.

1902   The school is their school and the coach must bear in mind that his is an extracurricular activity like glee clubs, debating societies, campus politics and publications.

1903   Never tell them how many letter men you'll get coming back. Tell them how many you lost.

Franklin C. "Pepper" Rodgers

Coach: Kansas 1967–1970, UCLA 1971–1973, Georgia Tech 1974–1979, Memphis Showboats (USFL) 1984–1985. Record: 111-103-3.

1904   I had only one friend, my dog. My wife got mad at me and I told her a man ought to have at least two friends. She agreed—and bought me another dog.

1905   Coaches like to talk about building character. They don't build character. They eliminate those who don't have it.

1906   I'm the only coach in history to go straight from the White House to the outhouse—*said after he got fired the day after meeting Jimmy Carter.*

Darryl Rogers

Coach: Hayward State 1965, Fresno State 1966–1972, San Jose State 1973–1975, Michigan State 1976–1979, Arizona State 1980–1984, Detroit Lions 1985–1988. Record 147-124-7.

1907   They'll fire you for losing before they'll fire you for cheating.

1908   I'm sure we'll screw it up before the season's over—*said after Lions won first two games in 1985.*

Darrell K. Royal

Coach: Edmonton Eskimos (CFL) 1953, Mississippi State 1954–1955, University of Washington 1956, University of Texas 1957–1976. Record: 201-65-5.

1909   Luck is what happens when preparation meets opportunity.

1910   A head coach is guided by this main objective: dig, claw, wheedle, coax that fanatical effort out of the players. You want them to play every Saturday as if they were planting the flag on Iwo Jima.

1911   No, we'll just dance with the one that brung us—*reply when asked if his team would do anything different in a big game.*

1912   It's a horse and a horse—*referring to a game involving two evenly matched teams.*

1913   The only place you can win a football game is on the field. The only place you can lose is in your hearts.

1914   I've never been kicked in the pants by anyone in front of me.

1915   I was as nervous as a pig in a packing plant.

1916   It makes them look wiser than a treeful of owls—*referring to ABC executives, who asked for, and got, the universities of Texas and Alabama to reschedule a game at the end of the season. By that time, both teams had impressive records, resulting in more interest in the contest.*

1917   We were outpersonneled.

1918   Breaks balance out. The sun don't shine on the same old dog's rear end every day.

1919   I thought God was neutral—*said after seeing church sign urging congregants to pray for Texas opponent.*

1920   What the heck does this place have? A low per capita income and pig farmers—*referring to Alabama.*

1921   Once you're across the fifty, you feel like an unsaddled horse.

1922   You've got to be in a position for luck to happen. Luck doesn't go around looking for a stumblebum.

1923   We're scratched up a little, but we're not gushing blood.

1924   You can call in the dogs and piss on the fire now—*referring to his team's commanding lead near the end of a game.*

Sam Rutigliano

Coach: Cleveland Browns 1978–1984, Liberty University 1989– . Record: 54-55.

1925   For a team to be successful, it must have a solid core of veterans to provide leadership.

1926   I don't swing from a chandelier one week and come crawling under a rug the next—*referring to his even-handed personality and stable philosophy.*

1927   Our main purpose with the passing game is to throw the ball effectively in order to open up our running game. Without the thrust of the pass our running game can easily be stopped. We would like to gain control of each game by running the ball; therefore, we must be able to pass.

James D. "Buddy" Ryan

Coach: Philadelphia Eagles 1986– . Record: 33-31-1.

1928   I didn't know who had the ball or what the hell was going on—*referring to a game played in pea-soup fog against Chicago in 1988.*

1929   All these guys walking out, there must be some really good paying jobs out there that I don't know about—*referring to players walking out of camp over disputes.*

Lou Saban

Coach: Case Institute 1950–1952, Northwestern 1955, Western Illinois 1957–1959, Boston Patriots 1960–1961, Buffalo Bills 1962–1965 and 1972–1976, Denver Broncos 1967–1971. University of Miami 1977–1978, Army 1979. Record: 148-142-10.

1930   I always look for more difficult challenges. I'm not sure I can find them any more difficult than here. You've got to understand, this is the bottom—*said when, at age 66, he started coaching at South Fork High School, Stuart, Florida, where team had been 1–9 last two seasons.*

1931   When we scored the winning TD, Bobby was all over me yelling, "Great chaps! Great chaps!" Then he took off for the end zone and started pounding the players and congratulating them. We had to chase after him all the way down to the end zone and tell him to get in there and kick the extra point—*referring to employing foreigners, such as Englishman Bobby Howfield, as kickers.*

1932   I didn't know about it until they phoned me—*referring to his firing by the Patriots.*

Henry R. "Red" Sanders

Coach: Vanderbilt 1940–1943 and 1946–1948, UCLA 1949–1957. Record: 102-41-3.

1933   He who lives by the pass, dies by the pass.

1934   I'm prejudiced in favor of any boy who can play football and intolerant of any player who won't block and tackle—*reply when asked about his attitude about race.*

1935   If you don't like him, I'm pretty sure you wouldn't like me—*said to a student athlete who asked about transferring to UCLA because he didn't like his present coach.*

1936   They were so quiet, it was as if a world convention of undertakers had just been informed that somebody had really discovered the secret of eternal life—*referring to his opponent's fans when UCLA scored a touchdown.*

1937   I'm too busy coaching them to court them—*referring to why he didn't become pals with players.*

1938   We've got an impossible, hypocritical aid code out here that nobody can live by and nobody's really trying to—*said in 1950.*

1939   The only thing worse than finishing second is to be lying on the desert alone with your back broke. Either way, nobody ever finds out about you.

1940   The worst mistake a coach can make is to get caught without material.

1941   I can't put in what God left out; I am no miracle man.

John Sandusky

Coach: Baltimore Colts 1972. Record: 4-5.

1942   There's only one game where "close" counts—horseshoes.

1943   He gets things done with his feet and mind, but he looks so unlike a super-athlete that people mistake him for an assistant personnel manager, maybe, gone to seed and living high on the hog—*referring to Dan Sullivan.*

1944   His nickname was "Fatso." He was fat. He couldn't run the 40-yard dash if you gave him from ten in the morning till two in the afternoon. He was always being kidded about it. But what a fine player—quick, strong and great balance. No one could knock him off his feet. You very seldom saw him on the ground—*referring to Dan Sullivan.*

Glenn E. "Bo" Schembechler

Coach: University of Miami 1963–1968, University of Michigan 1969–1989. Record: 234-65-8.

1945   There's a slight difference, but it's not that much—*referring to recruiting baseball, as opposed to football, players—said after becoming president of the Detroit Tigers after leaving Michigan.*

1946   I may have some different ideas that may be contrary to how baseball normally is run.

1947   I coached from the heart and from the throat. The kids in my program know that when they come to practice they better be 100 percent ready or they're going to hear about it.

1948   I'd kick you in the butt, but I'm afraid I'd lose my foot.

1949   I have practice—*said to George Bush when the future president asked for his help while campaigning in Grand Rapids.*

1950   The mess in athletics isn't only caused by crooked college coaches.

1951   In the years I worked under him, I fought with the man, argued with him, went home at night and cursed him. But, oh, how I learned under him—*said about Woody Hayes, whom he worked for as assistant coach at Ohio State.*

1952   When you're on the sidelines, you don't have time to worry about being polite.

1953   We're at war out there.

1954   Football coaches screaming in smoke-filled rooms are like kids playing in the mud. The joy is in getting dirty—*said about staff meetings.*

1955   A guy throwing his body around and hurting people, that's an unnatural thing. It has to be instilled at around the junior high school level.

1956   I do not care if you are white or black or Irish or Italian or Catholic or Jewish or liberal or conservative. From this point I will treat you all exactly the same—like dogs.

1957   I made them suffer every day of that first maddening season.

1958   Sometimes you have to scare the crap out of them. Sometimes you have to lead by example. Sometimes you just have to get out of the way.

1959   As a coach, I am the consummate actor.

1960   Motivation. It is, quite simply, the spark that makes someone do that which he might not otherwise do.

1961   Motivation. It is the transference of your heart and soul into your players' minds and bodies.

1962   Nothing motivates like your own failure.

1963   If a football coach succeeds in a football crazy town, he can have carte blanche.

1964   You will never get the same level of effort from one man seeking glory as from a group of men pulling for a shared goal.

1965   Somewhere beneath that crusty exterior, you must be human. I will not hesitate to cry in front of my team.

1966   I will never prepare a speech; whatever comes out, comes out.

1967   They're my alter ego during a game. I want them to think like me, react like me—*referring to quarterbacks.*

1968   This was a lonely guy—*said of Elvis Presley.*

1969   My favorite thing in football is probably an 80-yard drive in which I've shown some dominance up front, opened up some big holes, made some beautiful blocks and on the final play, from inside the five, we knock it home. That's football to me.

1970   . . . combat without weapons.

1971   The game has exploded. It's big money. It's big pressure. It's out of control.

1972   The whole attraction was money and that's no reason to take a job—*referring to why he turned down a position.*

1973   Hey listen, I don't need them if I win and they can't help me if I lose—*referring to sportswriters.*

1974   Defense wins games.

1975   You get tired of the damned things unless you're the guy kicking them—*referring to field goals.*

1976   The problem with the field goal is that it rewards penetration by allowing you three points when you are not in the position to score six. That's not inherently bad. But when you only have to cross the 50-yard line to do it, then it doesn't make sense. And that's where we are headed.

1977   It's so damned frustrating to bang bodies with the opponent, down after down, knocking open holes, slamming holes shut, then, on fourth down, have the game decided by everyone watching a ball sail over their heads.

1978   I have coached thousands of college football players, scared them, inspired them, broken them down and built them back up. I've become famous for screaming, for temper tantrums, for never failing to have an opinion. And now, in the sterile hospital room, I could think of nothing comforting to tell my wife—*referring to going in for heart surgery.*

1979   I'm not opposed to women sportswriters. I'm opposed to them being in the locker room. Frankly, I'm opposed to all sportswriters being in the locker room.

1980   Losing tears the heart out of you and I don't have a good one to begin with.

1981   I'm here to put a hustling, entertaining team on the field and win championships. I'm a healthy man. I think I've got another decade in me—*said after he left Michigan to became president of the Detroit Tigers.*

1982   It's like Disneyland. You've got to understand you're in the entertainment business—*referring to baseball.*

1983   I don't want any tribute. Get rid of it—*said to bandmaster at the University of Michigan, who was planning to honor the departed Schembechler with a halftime show at the school.*

Joseph P. "Joe" Schmidt

Coach: Detroit Lions 1967–1972. Record: 43-35-7.

1984   Life is a shit sandwich and every day you take another bite.

1985   I am not willing to make my family number two to get to the Super Bowl—*referring to why he resigned from the Lions.*

1986   You guys whip Notre Dame or so help me, I'll whip you—*said to his teammates during his college days at the University of Pittsburgh.*

1987   I want to win, and in football a coach only has fourteen chances during the season to do it. A baseball coach has a hundred and sixty-two games on his schedule. In football, you cannot lose.

1988   There's nothing worse than walking across a field towards a locker room if you've lost, and nothing better if you've won.

1989   I don't enjoy it as much as I used to. I still have a sense of humor, but I don't show it as much as I used to.

1990   I remember during that first season I came out on the front steps and found the Monday trash spread all over my front lawn, and the garbage cans overturned. We'd lost a game that weekend, and I was paranoid enough to think that some fans were responsible—and this was their way of being critical. I stomped around wanting to pop somebody. Then I found out that it was our dogs.

1991   The greatest horror of coaching is losing.

Floyd B. "Ben" Schwartzwalder

Coach: Muhlenberg College 1946–1948, Syracuse University 1949–1973. Record: 178-96-3.

1992 Football is not a democracy on the field. We have rules and you look upon yourself as a kind of benevolent dictator.

1993 The alumni wanted a big name coach and got a long name coach—*referring to when he got his job at Syracuse.*

1994 A successful coach is one who is still coaching.

1995 I tried to coach my players as if they were my children, and Dad's got to be tough with his kids once in awhile.

1996 If I cussed out a kid, it never got personal. I'd call him a bum or something, but I'd keep it on a high level. I never used that much profanity. When it was all over, if I'd been a little rough on a kid, I'd always put my arm around him. You know, you don't carry anything over beyond one day.

1997 You can't berate kids and build them up.

1998 We were always able to get a laugh day to day.

1999 Football coaches don't have too much chance to get fat-headed. That's because even if you're winning, someone will tell you that you're winning only because of the material you've got.

2000 There are very few arrogant coaches, particularly people who have been around for awhile. Like one coach told me, "Ben, we're like monkeys on a pulley. Some of us are going up and some of us are going down. We pass each other en route."

2001 I'd rather play the best and beat a few than play poor teams and beat them all.

2002 Boys, I think you'd better vote again—*said after team voted to go to the Orange Bowl instead of the Cotton Bowl, where it would have faced a tougher opponent. The team changed its mind.*

2003 Everybody advised me not to work the team too hard, and we didn't—*referring to his 61-6 loss at the '52 Orange Bowl to Alabama.*

2004 Well, I'd been up for 24 hours getting my outfit ready and I figured I needed some rest, because I wouldn't get it when I hit the ground—*referring to fact that he slept while crossing the English Channel on D day in World War II before parachuting down to combat.*

2005   We started with 170 men and 13 officers but at the end of 38 days we had left only 43 men and one officer—me—*referring to World War II at Normandy.*

2006   People always feel justified, you know, in finding fault with anything a coach does.

2007   I wonder how exciting our fans would think it was if we threw 40 or 50 passes every game but lost—*referring to comment that an upcoming opponent, Florida State, was an exciting team because it passed a lot. Syracuse beat them, 37–21.*

2008   Jim's outstanding attribute as a football player was his inde-structibility. Jim never missed a minute of play due to injury in three years of varsity ball. And he was always the fellow the other club was gunning for—*referring to Jim Brown.*

2009   The blood was running down into his eye and I wanted to take him out, but he said, "I can still see the goal line"—*referring to Jim Brown.*

2010   I was tired of him. He just walked off. But I was told by people that I had to take him back. They didn't care what concessions I had to make—*referring to Jim Brown, who broke rules.*

2011   He doesn't pass left-handed and his mother didn't have twins—*reply when asked for criticisms of Floyd Little.*

2012   When you talk about Ernie Davis, you're treading on hallowed ground. We always thought he had a halo around him and now we know he has—*said at time of Davis' death of leukemia at age 23. Davis was first black man to win Heisman Trophy.*

2013   Each was great in his own right—*reply when asked to pick the best of three Syracuse players.*

2014   Before the talk, the team was a unit. After that, it was two groups, one white, one black. If I had known what was going to happen I would have refused to hold that stupid meeting—*referring to racial tension on the team in '68.*

2015   I got hauled off to this meeting with three fellows who're supposed to represent the black players. They were one-half hour late and when they got there they started telling me this and that.

2016   You've got to be a sociologist now, not a coach.

2017   So it wasn't too good to have wound up on a bad note. Except that I worked harder and I became a better coach because of having to deal with adversity. What is winning and losing? Everything is relative—*said upon leaving job.*

2018   I get mad, but if people that I deal with are emotional young men—and I know they will do things that maybe they shouldn't do—as long as they hustle and behave themselves and they want to contribute to the team effort, I'll listen to them. My doors have never been shut.

2019   Coaches—and fans—should be mindful that when a team lines up against its equal, the basic fundamentals pay off. If you're solid basically, you can afford the luxury of a cute wrinkle or two. But you don't ever beat a good football team just by fooling them.

2020   The timing on the Patriot offer was bad. I never really had a chance to think about it. They came down to talk, and I had to decide before the game. Well, I just couldn't think of Boston at that time. I told them, "If you gotta know, before the game, then it's no good." It was a good offer, too. At that time the money they wanted to give me was something. I'd have a five-year contract, a house, a car, the works. And my wife wanted me to take that job. Well, actually I was kind of an idiot that I didn't take it because I would have security.

Mike Shanahan

Coach: Los Angeles Raiders 1988–1989. Record: 8-12.

2021   As soon as you lose, everybody wants you to change quarterbacks.

2022   I wish I could have given some Knute Rockne speech. I just said I was embarrassed and that there was a lot of pride at stake. We just had to play our game—*referring to halftime locker room talk when team was down 27–3. It went on to tie Denver, 27–27, during regulation play and win by field goal in overtime.*

Dr. Albert "Al" Sharpe

Coach: Cornell 1912–1917. Record: 34-21-1.

2023   I think that the scheme of numbering the men will aid the officials in the exchange of their duties and will help the spectators follow more closely the intricate plays of the game—*said in 1913.*

Clark D. Shaughnessy

Coach: Tulane 1915–1920 and 1922–1925, Loyola of the South 1926–1932, University of Chicago 1933–1939, Stanford 1940–1941, University of Maryland 1942 and 1946, University of Pittsburgh 1943–1945, Los Angeles Rams 1948–1949. Record: 163-113-17.

2024   Couldn't I just leave $500 here on deposit? — *said after standing in line a long time to pay one of many tickets for driving violations.*

2025   I love to try things. In fact, I always have a tendency to try too much. I usually throw out about three-quarters of everything I work out.

2026   If a coach dares try something new and it flops, he gets fired because he's a screwball and only a stupid person would attempt such a thing. But if he tries something that's been successful with another team and it fails, he's got a perfect out. He can blame it on his material, and keep his job, particularly if he's a good apple-polisher.

2027   By the time you get a player on a professional team, his character has already been formed. The only thing I can do as his coach is teach him what I know about the subtleties of the game, things he may not have learned in college because the college coach was too busy teaching him fundamentals. I don't have time to teach fundamentals and I have to assume the player comes to me with all his tools sharp. I have to show him the best ways to use them.

2028   If he didn't have desire and courage, he wouldn't be here. Remember, when he went to college, he usually went on a scholarship and that meant he had been picked as one of the best high school players in his area. If he played well enough in college to be drafted by a pro team, then he had survived another stage in the weeding-out process. If he was drafted, it means he was considered one of the best 360 senior college football players in the United States. Then, if he makes the team, just the roster, he's passed the final test for his Ph.D. There's nothing I can do for his personality or his character or his desire to play football. All of that has already been done. Only the best survive and all I can do is polish them.

Lawrence T. "Buck" Shaw

Coach: North Carolina State 1924, University of Nevada 1926, Santa Clara 1936–1942, University of California 1945, Air Force Academy 1956–1957, San Francisco 49ers (AAFC) 1946–1954, Philadelphia Eagles 1958–1960. Record: 119-74-12.

2029   The first guy who goes out there and purposely tries to hurt

Graham is off the team—*referring to Otto Graham, who played for the Eagles'*
opponents, the Browns.

Alex "Allie" Sherman

Coach: Winnipeg Blue Bombers (CFL) 1954–1956, New York Giants 1961–1968.
Record: 85-82-7.

2030   The strategy of trying to outguess and outwit the opponent is
football at its finest.

2031   Sheer power is physical strength and muscular prowess. Deception is mental overpowering plus prowess.

2032   In 1959, when I was backfield coach for the Giants, we opened
eight straight ball games with a long pass on the very first play. It was a
shocker and a surprise in the first game, to be sure, but the fact that we continued with it was even more shocking and surprising. Every opponent was
certain we wouldn't do it more than once, or twice, or three, or four times,
let alone eight straight opening passes. In three of those eight games we got
a touchdown on that first play.

2033   Football is supposed to be so creative, innovative—conceptually,
formation-wise, tactically—yet it's got a great deal of imitation. If a guy hits
with a style, people take it and try to understand why.

2034   I listen when people have a suggestion because I know there's
always the possibility of learning something.

2035   You always want to play to the strong man. He's going to defeat
you if you try to avoid him. The more times you go at him, the better chance
there is of making him break down.

2036   I loved it, the whole scene. I'd watch films at one in the morning
with (Greasy) Neale, and I was absorbing things: percentage moves, how
to evaluate defense, how to evaluate offense. And my mother used to say,
"What kind of business is this for a Jewish boy?"

2037   If I go back to bed, I might forget the play—*reply after waking*
up his head coach, Greasy Neale, in the middle of the night to explain a new play
and being told, "Go back to bed."

2038   I never heard "Jewboy." But they did make fun of my New York
accent.

2039   This ball club here was predominantly Texan for several years.

I gotta live football—that's my job—so I think it was only natural that I started talking like the men I was more or less living with—*referring to his days as assistant coach with the Giants.*

2040   A play is always perfect when it works.

2041   There are no overnight personal success stories in football.

2042   A defensive end is like a shepherd and the offensive players are his sheep.

2043   Football is war. The coach is the general; the quarterback, the commanding officer; the players, the soldiers.

2044   You can't be dumb and a good football player. At least on my team you can't.

2045   God! Retired at 25½!—*said when he retired from playing with the Eagles to coach the Patterson Panthers in the American Association in 1948.*

2046   Jewish people out of New York are more clannish. They're a minority and they're going to want to dominate all your time. But you're not in Winnipeg representing the Jewish faith. You're the head football coach's wife and I'm the head football coach—*said to his wife when he joined Winnipeg.*

2047   I honestly believe football will give me everything I want but you've got to take a ride with me on it—*said to his wife in Winnipeg after he turned down a few assistant coaching jobs in the USA, refusing to accept anything except a head coaching position.*

2048   I shut the door, locked it and then started to talk to them. "Guys," I said, "there are three men on this team who can decide the future of the rest. We can win a championship or we can be broken into factions and cliques and bicker back and forth all season. The three men are in this room right now. I need your help. I am in my first year as coach.... But I'm going to have to make a big decision and I want you both to understand. I am going to have to pick one of you as my starter and I don't know when I can make that decision. It might be in a week or it might not be until the middle of the season. All I ask is that the both of you be ready to play, be prepared to play and be prepared to sit on the bench. I know that's a lot because you've both been starters for a long time, but the Giants can win a championship if I make the right choice, and I'll need all your help and understanding to make that choice and stick with it. Okay?"—*said to Y.A. Tittle and Charlie Conerly.*

2049   In pro football you begin with the quarterback. If you have a good one, you've in business. If you don't, you're dead.

2050   A quarterback should learn to think with his feet as well as with his brain.

2051   Many a quarterback's hopes are kept alive with the ever-present thought, "If we can only advance that ball to field goal position, we'll still have a chance."

2052   No matter how great a player is in college, when he reports to the pro leagues for the first time, he's a rookie.

2053   What's my inventory? The human element is my inventory.

2054   When you lose, you've got to know why you lost.

2055   Be fair to yourself.

2056   In the theater, if a play gets bad enough notices from the critics, it closes after one performance. The football coach isn't that lucky.

2057   All the gold fixtures in the bathroom won't mean a thing if the plumbing's no good.

2058   No matter how old or how big you are or what position you play or what your level of ball is—backyard, sandlot, Pop Warner Conference, little league, high school, college or pro—you, the player, are the unknown quantity in football.

2059   A coach should go with the tools he has. The plays must be built around his players, not his players around the plays.

2060   Football is like boxing. If you get hit once where it hurts, you protect yourself so you don't get hit there again.

2061   The fringes, the endorsements, the TV shows, all of this—it's a plus. But in turn, it can become a minus. Too much exposure can wear a man down physically and soften him up. Because why? Because now he's not scratching.

2062   There are three ways to do anything, the right way, the wrong way and your way.

2063   The mind or body can only absorb so much.

2064   In football, nothing is left to chance except the outcome of the game itself.

2065   One of the hardest lessons we have to learn is how to lose gracefully and win gracefully, too.

2066   The immediate problem. Resolve it. Go at it. A problem that's foolish to attack right now. Wait a week or two or three. A problem that's in sight but one that you have to let solve itself—*referring to his three categories of problems.*

2067   A team must have a soul.

Jackie Sherrill

Coach: Washington State 1976, University of Pittsburgh 1977–1981, Texas A&M 1982–1988. Record: 105-45-2.

2068   Football is a business. Let's get our heads out of the sand.

2069   We've been practicing in 105-degree temperature and down on the turf I figure it's around 140 degrees.

Donald F. "Don" Shula

Coach: Baltimore Colts 1963–1969, Miami Dolphins 1970– . Record 285-132-6.

2070   Winning is the ethic of football. You start with having to win and you work back.

2071   The important thing is not what Don Shula knows or what any of my assistant coaches know. The important thing is that we can transmit to the people we're responsible for.

2072   That's what coaching is—the ability to transmit information.

2073   Almost nothing has changed. From one year to the next, the schedules are the same; we work on the same things at the same time. I'm not sure if that's good or bad.

2074   To me, coaching is finding out what makes an individual play to the best of his ability. I have to understand how best to motivate each and every one, and of the 45 players I'm going to be responsible for this year, there are no two alike.

2075   You kick some in the butt, praise others, continue to harass a third group. They're all different and you've got to realize this.

2076   When we got the ball it was up to us to grind it out. We had third and four, and if we missed on this fourth down the Vikings would have one last shot at a touchdown or a field goal. The Vikings looked for a short pass, and they went to double coverage on our prime receivers. And Johnny, in a typical Unitas move that combined intelligence, quick analysis of a defense with the daring to call an unorthodox play, called a quarterback draw. He dropped back in the pocket and cocked his arm and the pass defenders flew out of there. Then he tucked the ball under his arm and ran up the hole in the middle for the first down.

2077   The higher you pick, the tougher the screening must be. With the higher picks, there is more money, more everything involved.

2078   I've tried to learn from all and copy none.

2079   The leader must call the shots and he must accept whatever consequences result. A lot of times those shots aren't popular but the thing I've found is that you must sit down with a guy, eyeball-to-eyeball, tell him what you're doing and why you're doing it. Even though he doesn't accept it, even though it might affect him in a negative way, he'll wind up respecting you and even talking to you later on and praising you for doing it.

2080   Sell me. Don't quit because I'm not interested the first time you present something.

2081   By admiring and respecting an opponent, I think you get a tremendous desire to whip them.

2082   The story of the game was simple. We didn't do it and they did — *referring to Colts loss to Jets in '68 Super Bowl.*

2083   Uncorrected errors will multiply. Someone once asked me if there wasn't benefit in overlooking a small flaw. I asked him, "What's a small flaw?"

2084   Misdirection makes those defensive linemen hesitate. If they know what you are doing, they are so big and quick they are going to destroy you. But if we can get them to wait and look—where they are not sure what they are doing—we have the advantage.

2085   If you want to rest your team, you don't have to give them time off, just cut down on the physical activity — *referring to his use of "walk throughs" in practice, when players walk through plays instead of running hard.*

2086   Yeah, you lost one of your earrings — *reply to a player wearing one earring who asked, "Notice anything, coach?"*

2087   Why do you think I go to Mass every day?—*explaining his luck in obtaining a good player still available after being passed over by 26 other teams—Dan Marino.*

2088   When we win, we know it's not final.

2089   I'm willing to answer the "why" question.

2090   The pass was so devastating for us. Boom, boom, boom and we were in the end zone.

2091   You play blind chess the second time around. You know what the other team has done and what you have done and you have to try to put yourself in the position of the other coach. You know he won't make the same mistakes, he knows you won't. You have to try to imagine what mistakes he will make compensating and what mistakes he thinks you will make.

2092   There is no single thing in a football game that turns the fortunes of the two teams more than a goal line stand.

2093   Once the season starts you have to be totally dedicated to the job. There's no other way.

2094   There are many benefits to a head coach's job, but the loss of family life is one of the negatives.

2095   After the victories, you can look back at all the hard work and laugh.

2096   He was very unselfish, probably the most unselfish of all the quarterbacks I've coached. He could care less if he threw a touchdown pass or handed off to Larry Csonka in a play that went for a touchdown. It was all a chess game to him—*referring to Bob Griese.*

2097   How do you tell a guy who led you to 11 straight victories that he was going to be benched?—*said about Earl Morrall, who was taken out when Bob Griese recovered from an injury.*

2098   I've never tried to take a system and jam it down a team's throat. I build my offensive and defensive game plans around the type of people we have to execute them.

2099   It was the lesser of two evils—*referring to when his team was on the one-yard line, leading 40–0, and it went for a field goal instead of a touchdown.*

2100   Monday is a long day for coaches and a day off for the players.

2101   What I don't know I could employ.

2102   A whole season—or a championship game—can turn on just one or two plays.

2103   He would wait until the last instant to release the football and paid the price. He put his neck on the line all the time, knowing he was going to take the big hit by waiting so long, but he gave Raymond Berry or Jimmy Orr an extra step to get open. He'd pick himself up, bleeding, off the ground and play the next play. He was one of the toughest guys I've ever coached—*referring to Johnny Unitas.*

2104   It took us a long time to lose our first game last year, but it didn't take long at all this year—*said after team lost first game of '85 season to Houston.*

2105   One of the big things I learned was never to assume anything. Always make sure you give complete details in the game plan and any specifics you want executed on the day of the game.

2106   In pro football you are supposed to follow protocol whenever you would like to hire an individual from another football team. You first contact the owner and ask permission to talk to the individual. Ownership goes to ownership.

2107   We stunk but they played a hell of a game.

2108   I don't mind working on Christmas and New Year's. Our goal is to get it all.

2109   The whole season has come down to one game—*referring to the Super Bowl.*

2110   Must be some nut calling at this hour—*said before answering 1:30 A.M. call from President Nixon before Super Bowl VI. Nixon wanted to suggest a play.*

Amos Alonzo Stagg

Coach: Springfield (Mass.) YMCA Training School 1890–1891, University of Chicago 1892–1932, College of the Pacific 1933–1946. Record: 314-197-35.

2111   Jim, I play you there because you can do the meanest things in the most gentlemanly way—*reply to a Springfield player who asked why he was chosen to be the center. The player was James Naismith, who later created basketball.*

2112   After much thought and prayer I have decided that my life can best be used for my master's service in the position you have offered—*part of his letter of acceptance of job at University of Chicago.*

2113   Coaching is the primary factor in football.

2114   How to be a good coach is just as much a mystery as how to be a good general or captain of industry. Like all other jobs above common labor and office routine, it requires a native gift, a feeling for the task, for success.

2115   In the group picture of our 1892 football squad, whiskers and moustaches grew almost as lushly as did goldenrod on the Chicago prairie.

2116   Our books showed $732.92 taken in, $633.33 paid out and 13 games played—*referring to 1892 season.*

2117   Clarence Herschberger was the first exceptional back and punter to appear at Chicago. He had made the team with a bang in 1894, his first season, but he was missing in 1895. His mother, alarmed at the injured roll reported by the newspapers, had refused to permit him to play....

2118   My salary was $2,500 a year.

2119   The game was too young and too weak for such a situation to be thought particularly unusual—*referring to fact that, although the coach, he played on Chicago's team in '92 and '93.*

2120   The mounted policeman who patrolled the park was attracted by the game. He happened to be galloping along the sidelines at the moment I made a touchdown and I still am accused of having used his horse as interference.

2121   We sold advertising space on the inner side of the fence, picking up ten dollars here and there. Our customers had to stand until the spring of 1894, when we built funny little bleachers that did not accommodate more than 150 persons.

2122   The first season the forward pass was legal, 1906, I personally had 64 different passing patterns.

2123   The tower pass was a Mutt-and-Jeff play. Two players, one tall, the other short and slight, dashed behind the enemy's goal line, the tall man lifted the little fellow in his arms, and little Jeff received a forward pass sent high over the defensive team's heads.

2124   We all love a winner. Not even a professional champion of lost causes can work up much enthusiasm over a college team that is trampled upon season after season.

2125   It is not necessary to cheat or to buy players in order to produce a team of which a school may be proud. A college with brains and courage, however small, does not need to hire a squad of mercenaries to wear its uniforms.

2126   Students are not fools. The faculty that winks at crooked work by a coach or student manager can save its breath in preaching ideals in the classroom.

2127   The whole tone of the game was smelly—*said after rejecting pro baseball contract because he objected to the sale of alcoholic beverages at games.*

2128   To me, our profession is one of the noblest and perhaps the most far reaching in building up the manhood of our country. As I view it, no man is too good to be the athletic coach for youth.

2129   My prayer has not been for victory. It has simply been, "Let me do my best."

2130   The loss of a game, however much you wish to win it, is not a tragedy but the manner of your losing may well be.

2131   A player must obey orders like a soldier when orders have been given and like a good soldier, act swiftly and surely on his own in an unforeseen contingency.

2132   I take my football very seriously but I try to preserve a sense of proportion.

2133   There are many men of superb imaginations in other respects whom football leaves cold.

2134   Mrs. Stagg was awakened one night by a violent tackle of her head. I had dreamed that I was falling on a fumbled football on the field. It is not unusual for a player to take the game to bed.

2135   Under the guise of fair play but countenancing rank dishonesty in playing men under assumed names, scores of professional teams have sprung up in the last two or three years, most of them on a salary basis of some kind. These teams are bidding hard for college players in order to capitalize not only on their ability but also and mostly on the name of the colleges they come from and in many cases the noised abroad mystery of their presence—*comment made about college men playing football for money using assumed names to hide their identities.*

2136   To cooperate with Sunday professional football games is to cooperate with forces which are destructive of the finest elements of interscholastic and intercollegiate football and to add to the heavy burden of the schools and colleges in preserving it in its ennobling worth—*comment made in 1923.*

2137   The day boys play with one eye on the university and the other on professional futures, the sport will become a moral liability to the colleges.

2138   If it is money that the college man wants he ought to be able to make more on a real job than by peddling a physical skill.

2139   Personally, I shall be a bit surprised if it succeeds—*referring to pro football.*

2140   I keep a tight reign on my emotions, the results of years of self-control. A coach must keep his mind on strategy, not the immediate score.

2141   Boys, you've got to win. John D. Rockefeller is in the stands—*Rockefeller gave a large endowment to the University of Chicago, where Stagg coached.*

2142   A hero is a man who takes a long chance and gets away with it; a goat is a man who risks all and loses all.

2143   Emotion is the unknown and highly explosive quantity in football and each coach is his own powder monkey.

2144   There are as many different methods of keying a team up to concert pitch for a game as there are coaches to do the tuning.

2145   I always hope that my teams can win without evangelism, but I never neglect that mental preparation. Before a big game I use every legitimate weapon I can command to rouse the heart, mind and temper of every man on the squad to a point where he can exert his supreme effort.

2146   It is not uncommon for coaches to curse their teams with everything in the index of profanity, both for its supposed goading effect and because many men cannot express themselves emphatically without recourse to profanity. For several reasons, I do not do it, and never have.

2147   Like all forms of overstatement, swearing is an opiate and progressively increasing doses are necessary for effect.

2148   Eleven men 100 percent in ability are too much to hope for but given a sizable squad any coach can see to it that he gets 100 percent in spirit.

2149   You may have 11 faster, heavier, headier men but the other fellow may land on you with intangibles that can't be shown on any form chart.

2150   Within its limitations, football is an art and players are born, not made.

2151   Certain physical attributes enter into being a football player, but a manufactured tackle or fullback will remain an automaton, a mechanical piano.

2152   A coach is a semipublic character and legitimate mark for criticism and advice.

2153   No, I have to live with my conscience. Let the kids work it out themselves—*said in the last few seconds of a game, when he refused to send in a substitute with orders to run a special play, which was against the rules—and his team lost.*

2154   I would like to be remembered as an honest man.

2155   Listen, Stockyards, you know what field this is. This is Stagg Field. I own it. If you go through that gate you won't come back in except by paying to sit in the stands—*said to an angry player.*

2156   I refuse to be idle and a nuisance—*said in 1932 at age 70, after refusing retirement and a pension from the University of Chicago. He waited until the season was over to leave.*

2157   I'm not too old. And I can't see any sound reason for my quitting football. I know too much—*said when he began coaching College of the Pacific.*

2158   Nice running. Now that's the way you're supposed to hit that line—*said when he was 88 and getting up from being knocked down during practice by a 220-pounder.*

2159   I must be going to live forever, because very few die after 90.

2160   When you get to be my age, this is the way you look and this is the way you write—*comment made after his hundredth birthday, on the way he appeared in a photo he autographed with a shaky hand.*

2161   Live in a way that makes you feel good and get your fun out of feeling good.

2162   Score the first touchdown and keep scoring.

Cal Stoll

Coach: Wake Forest 1969–1971, University of Minnesota 1972–1978. Record: 54-55.

2163   This year we've got Nebraska right where we want them — off the schedule.

Henry L. "Hank" Stram

Coach: Dallas Texans/Kansas City Chiefs 1960–1974 (team moved and changed name after 1962 season), New Orleans Saints 1976–1977. Record: 136-100-10.

2164   It's only a game when you win. When you lose, it's hell.

2165   Getting past him is like taking a trip around the world — *referring to 300-pound tackle Sherman Plunkett.*

2166   Yesterday is a canceled check, today is cash on the line, tomorrow is a promissory note.

2167   We hadn't used it for the last two months so it wasn't on the films — *referring to why end-around play was so effective in a game.*

2168   It's a game of people, not of notebooks.

2169   If a team doesn't have a good punter and kicker, it's in trouble. Look at the teams that have been successful through the years. They've had three things: a quarterback, good defense and the kicking game. I have seen too many fine teams with excellent offenses and defenses blow a game on a punt return, a blocked field goal or a weak punt.

2170   We don't have an overabundance of rules and regulations, but the ones we have will be followed to the letter.

2171   We respect every team we play.

Joseph L. "Joe" Stydahar

Coach: Los Angeles Rams 1950–1952, Chicago Cardinals 1953–1954. Record: 22-29-1.

2172   Fight for them, you bastards — *said as he threw paychecks to group of Chicago Cardinal players in locker room.*

2173   You son of a bitch, you go home and your wife will kill you. If you don't have the moxie to stick it out, you'll never amount to anything. Promise me you'll stay another week, and we'll decide whether or not you're good enough to play with us — *said to Andy Robustelli in 1951.*

2174   No wonder you guys get kicked around. Every one of you's still got his teeth—*said before the adoption of mandatory face masks.*

2175   No, you get your ass over here, and that goes for the rest of the team—*said over the phone to a player who found a swinging party, called the hotel where the Rams were staying, thought he was speaking to a teammate and said, "Get your ass over here."*

Dr. John B. "Jock" Sutherland

Coach: University of Pittsburgh 1918 and 1924–1938, Lafayette 1919–1923, Brooklyn Dodgers 1940–1941, Pittsburgh Steelers 1946–1947. Record: 172-44-15.

2176   Gentlemen, we have a problem. We have nine players too many and that issue has to be decided today. Put your hats on and get to work—*said to players on Pittsburgh Steelers right after WWII.*

2177   No coach sure of his team constantly bawls out his athletes.

2178   Speed is not your fastest but your slowest man.

2179   Count your sophomores and figure each one will cost you one or more touchdowns per season.

Harland Svare

Coach: Los Angeles Rams 1962–1965, San Diego Chargers 1971–1973. Record: 21-48-5.

2180   It was the most amazing thing I've ever seen. He'd never been to a single team meeting, but he shifted into every one of our formations as if he'd been running them all his life. He didn't miss one. Then he started running the plays as if we'd designed them especially for him; every time he got his hands on the ball he broke through the line. Gene, this is the best performance I've ever seen on a football field—*referring to Duane Thomas.*

2181   He stood about two inches away from me, face to face, nose to nose, and he just stared at me. He never said a word, he just stared. Then he left. It was scary—*referring to Duane Thomas.*

2182   An NFL coach is the big apple. I mean, your ass is really hanging in the breeze.

2183   I want you to really see the game, not like on television—toy size. Some damn expert telling you what you saw. Living room observers sitting around talking about what somebody should have done like it was a chess game instead of war. I want you down on the field where you can feel the hits, feel the ground shake. I want you in the locker room to hear the guys talking in there—no man's land, their camp. No women. Just men together getting ready. I want you to see the planning, the summer camp, the drafting, the coaches' meetings, the whole thing. You don't know anything about it. Nobody who hasn't seen it up close knows anything about it.

2184   Ninety percent of the game is in the mind.

2185   I guess part of me doesn't want to go to the stadium at all this morning. Another part feels alive—like a high. You know, like a general leading a band of outnumbered troops. I guess the risk turns me on. It's all on the table. Heads or tails. Life or death. Job or no job. Where else but in this nutty game can you have a fix like that and know you'll at least live through it.

2186   You never know whether a team is going to be up for a game until they're out on the field for at least a quarter.

2187   The league's attitude about dealing with the drug problem reminds me how my father dealt with sex. Mean looks and lots of no talk about it.

2188   The head is really the important professional football organ, but it all goes through the feet.

2189   The people who desperately need more and more, what shall I call it, action, get to the top of any bunch of guys. You know, companies, teams, armies, what have you. That kind of restless urge to escape from a feeling of nothing. They just got to. I've seen it up and down the ladder. But do you know another thing I've noticed about these action freaks? Once they get into the big games, the little games don't work anymore. They can't get a fix from a littler version of the game. Like from a chess game instead of a war. So their thing has to get bigger and bigger. I mean, we all play games. Some of us can keep it down to betting in a football pool or bowling on Saturday nights with the boys. Others have got to move armies, nations and even coach NFL football games.

2190   You know, I wondered whether or not to take the head coaching job. My wife and close friends all begged me to refuse. They reminded me that the general manager's job was secure. That I had already been fired once as the head coach of the Los Angeles Rams. Over and over they asked me why I wanted to risk it again. My wife even brought up the business about security for her and for our daughter, Mia. I guess I have a lot to prove. To myself and to everybody else in the game.

Barry Switzer

Coach: University of Oklahoma 1973–1988. Record: 157-29-4.

2191   Sometimes, even when you have the best players, you gotta be lucky.

2192   It was like a heart transplant. We tried to implant college in him but his head rejected it.

2193   I have never asked any coach to go out and offer an illegal inducement to any player.

2194   I swear it would scare people to death if they knew the frame of mind that those kids are in on the field.

2195   Football is a violent physical sport. It's a demanding sport run by demanding coaches who teach huge kids to collide into one another as fast as they can run.

Frank W. Thomas

Coach: University of Chattanooga 1925–1928, University of Alabama 1931–1942 and 1944–1946. Record: 141-33-9.

2196   Be a disciplinarian but not a slave driver.

Norman "Norm" Van Brocklin

Coach: Minnesota Vikings 1961–1966, Atlanta Falcons 1968–1974. Record: 66-100-7.

2197   Every defense is a little different. You've got to attack it a little different.

2198   There's no tougher way to make easy money than pro football.

2199   Never get in a kicking fight when you got the butt and the other guy's got the shoe.

2200   A quarterback should only run through sheer terror.

2201   All the good ones believe they can't drop the ball—*referring to pass receivers.*

W. Wallace "Wally" Wade

Coach: University of Alabama 1923–1930, Duke 1931–1941 and 1946–1950. Record: 171-49-10.

2202   The best you can do is not good enough unless it does the job.

2203   Nobody ever got back-slapped into winning anything.

Lynn O. "Pappy" Waldorf

Coach: Oklahoma City University 1925–1927, Oklahoma A&M 1929–1933, Kansas State 1934, Northwestern 1935–1946, University of California 1947–1956. Record: 174-100-22.

2204   I think we had 14 players out for the first practice, and I still remember about the fourth or fifth game, we played Southwestern Teachers at Oklahoma City, and we broke the school's record for gate receipts by taking in $87.50. That's what you call starting at the bottom—*referring to his first year coaching at Oklahoma City University.*

2205   Good players win games for you, not big players.

Douglas C. "Peahead" Walker

Coach: Atlantic Christian 1926, Elon 1927–1936, Wake Forest 1937–1950, Montreal Alouettes (CFL) 1952–1959. Record: 194-151-11.

2206   Oh, that was the West campus. You have to stay here at the East campus as a freshman—*said in the fall after he recruited a student that summer by showing him the beautiful Duke University campus in nearby Durham.*

2207   I decided it was time to quit when the Yankees made Casey Stengel manager. That was the job I should have had — *said when he retired from coaching minor league baseball.*

2208   I've tried winning. And I've tried losing. Winning's better.

Charlie Waller

Coach: San Diego Chargers 1969–1970. Record: 9-7-3.

2209   When I was made head coach I didn't have a projection room in my house to look at game and practice films. So I built an extra room and it cost me $20,000. Now that I'm not the head coach anymore, I've still got this room and I think you should pay me for it.

William E. "Bill" Walsh

Coach: San Jose (Continental League) 1967, Stanford 1977–1978, San Francisco 49ers 1979–1988. Record: 126-75-1.

2210   When you go into the playoffs, you start over. It's another season. Throw out scores and stats.

2211   There's no telling what we'll find when we raise the tarpaulin. A lot of fishing worms, I guess — *referring to Candlestick Park — comment made during rainy days before game in San Francisco.*

2212   Anytime you see a good old guy, a relaxed, unperturbed, steady guy, you're going to have a steady, mediocre team.

2213   I don't believe it's working the way we had hoped — *referring to the referees' use of instant replay.*

2214   We do everything but educate him. We're afraid he'll fail so we look for ways of making it easier — *referring to college athletes with poor academic records.*

2215   Quarterbacks have to be bright. They have to have instinctive awareness and they must keep a clear head under stress.

2216   With all of the specialty defenses around, offensive coaches have become more and more willing to run a series of plays to keep a given defense on the field. In other words, if the nickel defense was on the field, and you thought you could run against it, you might try to keep it there by lining up with no huddle. Or, if you wanted to throw the ball two or three times against a basic defense, you might go without a huddle three times in a row. It can become very hectic for your offense when you attempt to do that, and the players become somewhat winded. But I see a value in it.

2217   We had a lot of respect for Atlanta going into the game. We needed more — *said after 49ers lost to Falcons, 34–17, in '88.*

2218   I took him about as far as a man can take a player, to the upper reaches of mediocrity.

2219   It's not the same NFL passing game anymore. What was once sophisticated in passing has become outdated. You have to now find more ways to disguise, and showing run in short yardage situations and then throwing long, showing run from your own end zone and then passing, having a full backfield and two tight ends with just one receiver wide and then hitting that receiver, is becoming a way to go.

Joseph "Joe" Walton

Coach: New York Jets 1983–1989. Record: 54-59-1.

2220   We blew a few things. It wasn't so much that we got beat physically as we got beat mentally.

2221   Rookies need all the practice time they can get.

2222   I'd have to believe that Mark single-handedly made sacking the quarterback a glamorous thing. He single-handedly made the NFL start keeping sacks as a meaningful statistic. He brought attention to it like no one before — *referring to Mark Gastineau.*

Glenn S. "Pop" Warner

Coach: University of Georgia 1895–1896, Cornell University 1897–1898 and 1904–1906, Carlisle Indian School 1899–1903 and 1907–1914, University of Pittsburgh 1915–1924, Stanford University 1925–1932, Temple 1933–1938. Record: 313-106-32.

2223   In 1908 I started this innovation having backs stand with one or both hands on the ground — *referring to the crouching stance at the line of scrimmage.*

2224   I am quite sure that I was the first coach in football to use the four and two line which is so commonly used by teams today. I started this offensive method in 1906.

2225   I firmly believe in dispensing with the Pavlova stuff and getting right down to the business at hand—that of gaining ground with the least possible fuss and feathers.

2226   We'll use about five plays ... two reverses, an off-tackle, a trap play or two and perhaps a pass. I promise not to use anything else but I won't tell you in what order I'll use them—*said to Syracuse coach Chick Meehan before Pittsburgh-Syracuse game.*

2227   You play the way you practice. Practice the right way and you will react the right way in a game.

2228   You can't play two kinds of football at once, good and dirty.

2229   There is no system of play that substitutes for knocking an opponent down. When you hit, hit hard.

2230   Contrary to general opinion, coaches do not run football from the bench. Practically all a coach can do when his team takes the field is to watch the players and make substitutions when one of them shows signs of exhaustion or becomes injured.

2231   If Stanford ever wins a single game with that crazy formation, you can throw all the football I ever knew into the Pacific Ocean—*said in 1941 of new T formation.*

2232   If their skill is about the same, I'll take the all-outer over the in-and-outer every time.

Alex Webster

Coach: New York Giants 1969–1973. Record: 29-40-1.

2233   We never lost a game. When the other team won, it was luck. When we won, it was just the way it was supposed to be. We figured when we lost, the game just wasn't long enough.

2234   The pressure grew as we lost. Television people were tough, newspaper people were tough. It got to the point where I was really scared. People would throw things at the bus, and at the Yale Bowl the fans yelled things at me I just can't repeat. Hell, if one guy says those things to me, to my face, I put the guy up against the wall and cripple him. But how can I take on fifty thousand of them? We needed extra police just to protect me. I decided, who the hell needs this? It was affecting my whole life—*NOTE: the Giants played home games at Yale Bowl in 1973 and 1974.*

George T. Welsh

Coach: Navy 1973–1981, University of Virginia 1982– . Record: 105-86-3.

2235   I couldn't have lived with myself if I'd tried to tie the game with a field goal—*said after being behind, 17–14, in '77 Army-Navy game, with clock running out, ball on Army one-yard line and fourth down, he called for a pass, which was incomplete.*

2236   If I couldn't get things going that year, I figured why stay?—*said when he left Navy.*

2237   I wanted to set a system to fit the player instead of forcing the players into the system.

2238   Dwell on the past and you'll lose an eye. Forget the past and you'll lose both eyes—*quoting a line from Solzhenitsyn's* Gulag Archipelago *to his team.*

Carol White

Kicking coach under head coaches Bill Curry and Bobby Ross. Georgia Tech 1985– . Record: 26-28-1.

2239   I know I'm the only female member of the American Football Coaches Association. To those folks who have never experienced coaching, it might seem a little strange. But I don't think the athletes have any problem with it.

2240   What would Vince Lombardi say? "If you can win with her, then do it."

2241   I had discipline and wanted to pursue it, so many of my skills were self-taught—*referring to her entry into coaching, which began when she started keeping football statistics for a high school whose football staff kept shrinking.*

2242   Many kickers come to me having practiced in different ways and I do not demand that they change. It's up to them to decide whether they're kicking up to their potential.

2243   All hell has broken loose—*referring to the publicity after she got her job.*

2244   I am not a feminist. I don't perceive myself as the flag-waving type. I am sharing valuable information.

2245   I think personality had something to do with it.

2246   It's a very tiring profession—*referring to coaching.*

2247   I'm working toward a doctoral degree in organizational behavior. My coaching career is really just a case of the tail wagging the dog.

2248   I have an opportunity to get my Ph.D. without going broke.

2249   I've found that people who are secure in their knowledge of football don't mind having a female on the staff.

2250   Get involved with keeping statistics, volunteer for summer camps and work in sports medicine. If you prove your competence, there will be accessibility whether you are a man or a woman—*advice to other women who want to do what she's done.*

2251   An assistant should reflect the coach's philosophy, not take the spotlight.

2252   I keep expecting to wake up and find that I was dreaming.

Charles "Bud" Wilkinson

Coach: University of Oklahoma 1947–1963, St. Louis Cardinals 1978–1979. Record: 154-49-4.

2253   You can motivate players better with kind words than you can with a whip.

2254   My proudest accomplishment in coaching is the quality of the individuals that went to school or the university and what they've done since they graduated from O.U.

2255   The foundation of a football team is leadership from within the squad itself. Coaches, to a degree, help individuals and the team develop physical skills and coordination, but the basic elements of character have usually been established in the hearts and minds of college men.

2256   There's nothing that gives a football team a greater feeling of unity than to rally strongly together and win after starting the game two touchdowns behind. A football team doesn't learn to know itself until it gets in trouble.

2257   It is a very axiomatic truth that you must, in practice, rehearse every situation that the player will face in a game and then repeat it until the player can react from rote memory rather than having to think.

2258   The ones who win are the ones who are willing to prepare.

2259   Oh, yeah, I think our record could be broken. Every record is made to be broken—*referring to Oklahoma's record of 47 straight victories.*

2260   At the end of the third quarter, I was willing to settle for a scoreless tie—*said in the game in which his team's record of 47 straight wins was broken by Notre Dame, who won 7–0.*

2261   Well, we couldn't go on winning forever.

2262   Last week you lost and you took it with lots of sportsmanship. But I don't think you ought to get carried away about being a good sport. Let's put your mind back on winning—*said after 47-game winning streak came to an end.*

2263   The best way to attain superb physical condition is to punish yourself in practice after you are already dead tired.

2264   Remember that it's been medically proven that when your body is telling you to quit, you have gone only half as far as you can go.

2265   Desire, spirit, effort—anything you want to call it—won for us today.

2266   Everyone has worked hard and that includes the boys who were playing and those who knew they wouldn't play.

2267   The willingness to hit harder than the other fellow, to go all out for something you want and believe in, is one of the great lessons of the game.

2268   I have never seen a team that played the game with such furious enjoyment.

2269   Nobody remembers the team that gets beat. Who did Caesar ever beat? You don't know, do you? Who did the Yankees beat all those years they won the World Series? The defeated teams aren't remembered. The world belongs to the people who win.

2270   Remember the majority of players on a football squad are dissatisfied. Of your 55 men, only 22 get to play much and only 11 are completely happy.

2271   When you win, you gain confidence in your judgment. When you lose, you do some soul-searching. The validity of your judgment is then not so apparent.

2272   When mental toughness has been rewarded by victory enough times, it adds up to the winning attitude or tradition, which is more important than personnel and coaching.

2273   He had integrity. He was completely fair, honest and the most thorough, hard-working individual I have ever known. I sincerely believe he was the greatest coach in football. His ten-year record at Minnesota prior to the war is unequaled. Yet there came a day when he was no longer wanted—*referring to Bernie Bierman.*

2274   No matter how successful he may be, every coach eventually reaches a point where a lot of people want somebody else.

2275   In college football you play under whatever circumstances exist at the time. If you win, you do so with humility. If you lose, you try to lose the same way.

2276   All I ask you to do is play as well as you can. That's all. If you'll just do that, I'd be the happiest guy in the world.

2277   The answer lies deep down in your own heart.

2278   They make their faking work because of their poise. With lots of people after you, it's hard to look lackadaisical, especially when some of them are 220-pounders.

2279   Drinking a beer won't hurt a player physically. But it is a chink in his moral armor.

2280   Life goes on. It's short. We don't have much time to do the things we want to do. About all there is to life is what you do with your opportunities.

2281   I have never subscribed to the view that the owners of professional athletics are in business philanthropically, only to provide good times for the American citizen. My experience is they are quite businesslike, almost ruthless.

2282   The only ones who never lose are the ones who never play.

George Wilson

Coach: Detroit Lions 1957–1964, Miami Dolphins 1966–1969. Record: 68-84-8.

2283   One interesting thing is that you begin to lose your zest for it after awhile. Take Bobby Layne. In his great years, when he was knocked over because someone missed a block, he'd shove a friendly elbow into the guy's ribs and tell him to forget it, that he could take it. The fellow'd think, "What a guy!" and the next time he'd do better—out of sheer respect for a quarterback who could take it. He'd block a bull elephant for Layne, or run through a brick wall for him. But then after awhile it wasn't so easy to take, and Layne began to say, "You son of a bitch, you missed your block." The players said Layne began to flinch. It wasn't that—he just lost his liking for it. So he chewed them out. That was all right if he was infallible, but no quarterback is, or ever could be and his players began to lose respect for him—and when that was gone, his capacity diminished at the same time.

2284   After awhile the coach can't take the losses out on himself. So he turns on his players. He forgets that his players are men. And also he forgets that once he was a player.

2285   I make it a point never to take my coaching home with me. My wife and my five children are my fans. A team's problems aren't a dinner table subject with us.

Bowden Wyatt

Coach: University of Wyoming 1947–1952, University of Arkansas 1953–1954, University of Tennessee 1955–1962. Record: 104-61-5.

2286   Take the shortest possible route to the ball and arrive in a bad humor—*reply when defensive back asked for advice.*

Samuel D. "Sam" Wyche

Coach: University of Indiana 1983, Cincinnati Bengals 1984– . Record: 54-55.

2287   I think what it says is that ownership can evaluate their staff on something other than the results on the scoreboard—*referring to management's decision to stick with its coaching staff after a 4–11 season in 1987. The next year the team went to the Super Bowl—and lost.*

2288   The six shooter ain't been loaded yet, we're gonna get better.

2289   One more loss and my IQ will fall back to where everyone thought it was last year.

2290   When you're under duress, you operate in near-panic.

2291   I'll never be stonefaced. The biggest difference between this year and my first year here is I'm just not allowing things to eat me up inside.

2292   I like gambling, taking chances; it's what life is all about.

2293   Your guts say, "Yeah, let's ram it to them one more time but your brain says, "No, get outta here and take the win." — *referring to game in which his team was leading with seconds to go and had the ball on its opponent's eight-yard line. Twice quarterback Boomer Esiason took the snap and fell to his knees.*

2294   Having differences only means we're both competitive and want to win — *referring to his relationship with Boomer Esiason.*

2295   The bottom line is statistics don't mean anything. Big plays and turnovers decide ball games.

2296   If you look at all the matchups, they out-match us in virtually every category, starting with the head coach, and they've got the edge by a long shot on that — *referring to chance against Bill Walsh and the 49ers in Super Bowl XXIII.*

2297   They'll be the guys with the big armor; we'll be the guys with the sandals and leather straps — *referring to the same game. Cincinnati lost.*

2298   The players wanted to break 60 — *referring to why he ordered a field goal with 21 seconds left in a game in '89 that he had clinched. The field goal was good, and his team beat the Houston Oilers, 61–7.*

2299   I couldn't get the cheerleaders to go in — *referring to the same game and reason for his team's high score.*

Fielding H. Yost

Coach: Ohio Wesleyan 1897, University of Nebraska 1898, University of Kansas 1899, Stanford 1900, University of Michigan 1901–1923 and 1925–1926. Record: 196-36-12.

2300   Hurry up. Hurry up. If you can't do it, I'll find the men that can. Hurry up. Hurry up.

2301   A punt, a pass and a prayer—*referring to his philosophy of play.*

2302   In 1901 we used spinners, reverses, double reverses, laterals, split backs—everything that is in the modern game except the forward pass.

2303   As to rules, we didn't violate any in those days. There weren't any rules.

2304   Yale was the first to have the true feeling of the game, a game which means spirit, body contact and team play, all the finest elements of competition.

2305   There are three things that make a winning football team: spirit, manpower and coaching. If you boys love Michigan, they've got the spirit, you see. If they'll turn out, that takes care of the manpower. I'll take care of the coaching.

2306   Football games are usually lost rather than won. That's why we prefer to let the enemy gamble with passes and trick plays in his own territory.

2307   Control kicking has won many games for us when we seem outclassed in manpower. By kicking the ball into the coffin corner, we keep the pressure on our opponents and sooner or later they fumble. An enemy fumble is as good as a 50-yard run.

2308   At Michigan we believe that position is more important than possession.

2309   You don't put morale on like a coat, you build it day by day.

2310   Some folks can drink and it doesn't harm them. But it doesn't do them any good. And we want to be good, don't we?

2311   I'd like to see every youngster in this country play football because the game teaches what every youngster needs—discipline, self-sacrifice, clean spirit, clean living, quick thinking and the knack of facing heavy pressure and still fighting on and on.

2312   You should have seen the actors they gave me for players—a bunch of ping-pong players and dancing boys. They couldn't even catch a football in a butterfly net—*referring to the time he went to Hollywood to act as technical adviser for a movie about football.*

Joseph M. "Joe" Yukica

Coach: Boston College 1968–1977, Dartmouth 1978–1983. Record: 97-64-2.

2313   Our faculty are tenured people, there's a contractual agreement. Why am I treated any differently?

Robert C. Zuppke

Coach: University of Illinois 1913–1941. Record: 131-81-12.

2314   You never can tell about a football game because the ball is a funny shape and it takes funny bounces.

2315   Often an All-American is made by a long run, a weak defense and a poet in the press box.

2316   In most colleges, the leading contact games are football, wrestling and dancing.

2317   Egotism is the anesthetic that deadens the pain of stupidity.

2318   An athlete should keep his feet as long as he can—his head, always.

2319   You may have a chance to make the team here—*said to Red Grange.*

2320   Football isn't meant to be played for money. Stay away from professionalism—*said to Red Grange.*

2321   I will never have another Grange, but neither will anybody else. They can argue all they like about the greatest football player that ever lived. I'm satisfied I had him when I had Grange.

2322   Why is it that just when you players are beginning to know something about football after three years, I lose you and you stop playing? It makes no sense. Football is the only sport that ends a man's career just as it should be beginning.

2323   You should have had five touchdowns. You didn't cut right on that one play—*said to Red Grange after a game in which he scored four touchdowns.*

2324   If you can't do anything well, try to become an executive.

2325   A painting is a creation and so is a football team. Just as an artist creates a picture on a canvas, a football coach creates a mobile image out of an array of raw physical masses. Just as paintings are made up of dabs and swabs of different pigments, so football compositions are an orderly conglomeration of different types of men in motion.

2326   The game of football is to college life what color is to painting. It makes college life throb and vibrate.

2327   Athletics and art both require endurance. It takes vigor to paint powerfully over every inch of a canvas. I can't imagine a sissy making a vital painting.

2328   An athlete is a fine piece of moving composition—a painting merely immobile composition that may depict movement.

2329   Why are not more athletes artists? Because they are rarely in an environment which encourages them.

2330   Nothing is sillier than the brawn-but-not-brain slur sometimes made about athletes.

2331   Football is not the only physical expression of a mental exercise: the great singer, the great pianist, violinist, the painter—all express their thoughts physically.

2332   Why shouldn't art be brutal when and if nature is brutal? Why shouldn't I paint the trees as they are? When I go into the forest, trees scratch and scrape me. Am I expected to come back and paint a lovely scene? Football is brutal, too. But brutes can't play it. The value of all paintings, whether in pigment or pigskin, lies in some degree to their resemblance to life.

2333   The huddle formation was first used by the University of Illinois in 1921–1922. This formation caused considerable controversy because of its deviation from the orthodox method of calling signals. At the time the huddle was introduced, the innovation was called the "Ring Around the Rosie" because the players arranged themselves in propinquity around the signal caller.

2334   I'm also a candidate for the presidency. Will anybody nominate me? *Before anybody can answer:* All right, I nominate myself. Why not pick a little guy like me, whom you can push around?—*what he said to become president of the Football Coaches Association.*

2335   Just the hair on my forearm—*reply when he was asked what he had up his sleeve.*

2336   Plays don't win. It's the men who carry out the plays.

2337   All quitters are good losers.

2338   I'm burning up inside. If I weren't I'd have been out of this game long ago.

2339   No athletic director holds his job longer than two unsuccessful football coaches.

2340   The hero of a thousand plays becomes a bum after one error.

2341   The undefeated team is not always the strongest team. It might be the luckiest.

2342   A football coach's main problem is that he is responsible to irresponsible people.

2343   It is foolish to claim that football is all good. There are both good and bad in the game, as there are in human beings. A thing that is all good is no good.

2344   I am Louis the Fourteenth and you are my court. After us, the deluge.

2345   Now I know you boys haven't a chance to win this game tomorrow but I want you to do me just one favor. Granting this favor means an awful lot to me personally. Old Doc will probably josh me a little after the game about how we were unable to stop them at any time. Now won't you do this? The first two times Minnesota gets the ball, I want you to stop them dead for three downs in each case, and after that I don't care what happens. Now won't you do this for me?

2346   We don't care how big or strong our opponents are, as long as they are human.

2347   The tough mug may have a trembling knee.

2348   Some backs run very fast in one spot.

2349   On the first down, play for a touchdown. On the third down, play for a first down.

2350   Nobody but a dead man can come out of the game—*what he said to starting eleven—1921—and he meant it.*

2351   Today I want to have some fun. Get beaten 100–0 if you want to, but have fun.

2352   Howard, you are a great coach but you'd be a greater one if you'd take a drink once in awhile. You'd have more imagination.... Well, I've just had two drinks and figured out three new plays—*said to Howard Jones.*

2353   There is no scrap in a scrapbook.

2354   It is easy to learn how to play football through the eye; it is far more difficult to learn by ear, by being told how to do things.

2355   They tell me that I should go around kissing babies and talking to poor boys to persuade them to send their sons to Illinois. And they say this is one of the duties of a modern coach. And I told them that if that was the duty of a modern coach, then I wasn't capable of being a modern coach.

2356   Aim at the stars. If you don't hit them, you'll land pretty high anyway.

2357   Never let hope elude you. That is life's biggest fumble.

Bibliography

Bill Alexander
  Cohane, Tim. *Great College Football Coaches of the Twenties and Thirties.*
New Rochelle, NY: Arlington House, 1973.
  Collier's. Oct. 9, 1937, p.11.
George Allen
  Life. Oct. 15, 1971, p. 40.
  Nation's Business. Sept. 1975, p. 44.
  Newsweek. Nov. 1, 1971, p. 54.
  New York Times Magazine. Sept. 16, 1973, p. 13.
  Sport. Sept. 1980, p. 15.
  Sports Illustrated. Jan. 6, 1969, p. 22; Sept. 7, 1970, p. 34; Oct. 25, 1971,
p. 71; Jul. 9, 1973, p. 74. Jan. 30, 1978, p. 18; Mar. 15, 1982, p. 30; Oct. 8,
1984, p. 50.
Eddie Anderson
  Cohane, Tim. *Great College Football Coaches of the Twenties and Thirties.*
New Rochelle, NY: Arlington House, 1973.
  Bright, Chuck. *University of Iowa Football: The Hawkeyes.* Huntsville, AL:
Strode, 1982.
Dana X. Bible
  Cohane, Tim. *Great College Football Coaches of the Twenties and Thirties.*
New Rochelle, NY: Arlington House, 1973.
  Collier's. Nov. 30, 1945, p. 16.
  Newsweek. Oct. 14, 1946, p. 98.
Bernie Bierman
  Cohane, Tim. *Great College Football Coaches of the Twenties and Thirties.*
New Rochelle, NY: Arlington House, 1973.
  Collier's. Nov. 9, 1935, p. 16.
  Literary Digest. Oct. 30, 1937, p. 24.
  University of Minnesota *Gopher Gazette.* Oct. 1976.
Earl Blaik
  Blaik, Earl with Tim Cohane. *You Have to Pay the Price.* New York, NY:
Holt, Rinehart & Winston, 1960.
  Blaik, Red. *The Red Blaik Story.* New Rochelle, NY: Arlington House,
1974.
  Cohane, Tim. *Great College Football Coaches of the Twenties and Thirties.*
New Rochelle, NY: Arlington House, 1973.

Collier's. Oct. 28, 1950, p. 18.

Look. Oct. 27, 1959, p. 48; Nov. 24, 1959, p. 114.

Saturday Evening Post. Oct. 11, 1941, p. 16.

Sport. Nov. 1950, p. 24.

Time. Dec. 7, 1953, p. 79.

Bobby Bowden

Sports Illustrated. Sept. 5, 1988, p. 50.

Paul Brown

Brown, Paul with Jack Clary. *PB, The Paul Brown Story.* New York, NY: Atheneum Press, 1979.

Collier's. Oct. 28, 1955, p. 66.

Saturday Evening Post. Dec. 12, 1953, p. 30.

Sport. Dec. 1986, p. 91.

Sports Illustrated. Aug. 12, 1968, p. 24; Sept. 15, 1969, p. 26; Oct. 20, 1975, p. 22.

Frank Broyles

Sports Illustrated. Nov. 8, 1965, p. 30.

Bear Bryant

Bryant, Paul W. and John Underwood. *Bear: The Hard Life and Good Times of Alabama's Coach Bear Bryant.* Boston, MA: Little, Brown, 1975.

Esquire. Sept. 1977, p. 88; Nov. 1980, p. 44; Jun. 1986, p. 67; Sept. 1989, p. 204.

Ford, Tommy. *Bama Under Bear: Alabama's Family Tides.* Huntsville, AL: Strode Publishers, 1983.

Herskowitz, Mickey. *The Legend of Bear Bryant.* New York, NY: McGraw-Hill, 1987.

Look. Nov. 16, 1965, p. 101.

New Yorker. Jul. 28, 1980, p. 26.

Newsweek. Nov. 12, 1979, p. 133.

Sport. Dec. 1986, p. 114; Sept. 1980, p. 30.

Sports Illustrated. Aug. 15, 1966, p. 52; Aug. 22, 1966, p. 26; Aug. 29, 1966, p. 26; Sept. 5, 1966, p. 28; Sept. 12, 1966, p. 98; Oct. 23, 1966, p. 68; Sept. 11, 1972, p. 88; Dec. 27, 1982, p. 24.

Time. Dec. 7, 1981, p. 68; Dec. 27, 1982, p. 80.

Jerry Burns

Sports Illustrated. Nov. 3, 1986, p. 106; Dec. 5, 1988, p. 72.

Wally Butts

Atlanta Constitution. Dec. 17–31, 1973.

Outlor, Jesse. *Between the Hedges: A Story of Georgia Football.* Huntsville, AL: Strode Publishers, 1973.

Saturday Evening Post. Nov. 20, 1954, p. 37.

Frank Cavanaugh

Cavanaugh, Frank. *Inside Football.* Boston, MA: Small, Maynard & Co., 1919.

Cohane, Tim. *Great Football Coaches of the Twenties and Thirties.* New Rochelle, NY: Arlington House, 1973.

Jimmy Conzelman
Saturday Evening Post. Oct. 30, 1937, p. 16; Nov. 5, 1938, p. 18; Oct. 19, 1946, p. 21.
Don Coryell
Sport. Nov. 1983, p. 66.
Sports Illustrated. Feb. 20, 1978, p. 18; Sept. 28, 1981, p. 40.
Stein, Joe and Diane Clark. *Don Coryell: Win With Honor.* San Diego, CA: Joyce Press, 1976.
Fritz Crisler
Cohane, Tim. *Great College Football Coaches of the Twenties and Thirties.* New Rochelle, NY: Arlington House, 1973.
Perry, Will. *The Wolverines: A Story of Michigan Football.* Huntsville, AL: Strode Publishers, 1980.
Duffy Daugherty
Daugherty, Duffy with Dave Diles. *Duffy: An Autobiography.* Garden City, NY: Doubleday, 1974.
Saturday Evening Post. Nov. 11, 1956, p. 37; Nov. 4, 1967, p. 84–87.
Time. Oct. 8, 1956, p. 66; Nov. 12, 1965, p. 75.
Robert Devaney
Newsweek. Oct. 4, 1965, p. 60.
Sports Illustrated. Sept. 13, 1971, p. 52.
Dan Devine
People. Sept. 11, 1978, p. 78.
Saturday Evening Post. Nov. 18, 1961, p. 63.
Sports Illustrated. Sept. 29, 1975, p. 14.
Time. Oct. 4, 1971, p. 60; Oct. 7, 1974, p. 80.
Mike Ditka
Ditka, Mike with Don Pierson. *Ditka, An Autobiography.* Chicago, IL: Bonus Books, 1986.
Esquire. Oct. 1988, p. 73.
People. Jan. 15, 1987, p. 73; Dec. 12, 1988, p. 73.
Sport. Aug. 1985, p. 44; Nov. 1988, p. 52.
Sports Illustrated. Dec. 16, 1985, p. 78.
Gilmour Dobie
Cohane, Tim. *Great College Football Coaches of the Twenties and Thirties.* New Rochelle, NY: Arlington House, 1973.
Bobby Dodd
Atlanta Constitution. June 13, 1986.
Dodd, Bobby. *Bobby Dodd on Football.* New York, NY: Prentice Hall, 1954.
New York Times. Dec. 30, 1984.
Thomy, Al. *The Ramblin' Wreck: A Story of Georgia Tech Football.* Huntsville, AL: Strode Publishers, 1973.
Time. Nov. 12, 1956, p. 83.
Vince Dooley
Seaman, Rosie Soto. *The Legend of Bill and Vince Dooley: Bowl Breaking Brothers.* Huntsville, AL: Strode Publishers, 1981.

Sports Illustrated. Dec. 26, 1988, p. 24.

Time. Jan. 12, 1981, p. 53.

LaVell Edwards

Salt Lake City Tribune. Feb. 18, 1990.

Sport. Dec. 1984, p. 64.

Utah Holiday. September 1985.

Forrest Evashevski

Look. Oct. 25, 1960, p. 107.

Saturday Evening Post. Nov. 6, 1954, p. 27.

Weeb Ewbank

Zimmerman, Paul. *The Last Season of Weeb Ewbank.* New York, NY: Farrar, Straus and Giroux, 1974.

Jake Gaither

Curry, George. *Jake Gaither, America's Most Famous Black Coach.* New York, NY: Dod, Mead, 1977.

Joe Gibbs

Saturday Evening Post. Oct. 1988, p. 54.

Sport. Feb. 1988, p. 30.

Sid Gillman

Saturday Evening Post. Oct. 8, 1955, p. 27; Oct. 24, 1959, p. 31.

Sports Illustrated. Feb. 1, 1988, p. 52.

Bud Grant

McGrane, Bill. *Bud, the Other Side of the Glacier.* New York, NY: Harper & Row, 1986.

Sports Illustrated. Sept. 13, 1976, p. 76.

Forrest Gregg

Time. Nov. 14, 1988, p. 14.

George Halas

Halas, George with Gwen Morgan and Arthur Veysey. *Halas by Halas: The Autobiography of George Halas.* New York, NY: McGraw-Hill, 1979.

Newsweek. Jun. 10, 1986, p. 98.

Saturday Evening Post. Dec. 6, 1941, p. 24; Nov. 23, 1957, p. 34; Nov. 30, 1957, p. 30; Dec. 7, 1957, p. 36.

Sports Illustrated. Dec. 5, 1977, p. 36.

Time. Jun. 7, 1968, p. 46.

Jim Hanifan

Sport. Sept. 1984, p. 71.

Dick Harlow

Cohane, Tim. *Great College Football Coaches of the Twenties and Thirties.* New Rochelle, NY: Arlington House, 1973.

Rappoport, Ken. *The Nittany Lions: A Story of Penn State Football.* Huntsville, AL: Strode Publishers, 1973.

Saturday Evening Post. Oct. 12, 1940, p. 24.

Woody Hayes

Brondfield, Jerry. *Woody Hayes and the 100-Yard War.* New York, NY: Random House, 1974.

Esquire. Aug. 1985, p. 39.

Life. Nov. 21, 1969, p. 51.

Newsweek. Nov. 29, 1954, p. 65; Nov. 25, 1974, p. 64.

Reader's Digest. Sept. 1977, p. 98.

Sports Illustrated. Sept. 24, 1962, p. 124; Oct. 19, 1964, p. 30; Nov. 11, 1968, p. 16; Dec. 2, 1968, p. 22; Nov. 11, 1968, p. 16; Sept. 9, 1974, p. 36; Mar. 23, 1987, p. 94.

Time. Dec. 6, 1968, p. 65.

Vare, Robert. *Buckeye: A Study of Coach Woody Hayes and the Ohio State Football Machine.* New York, NY: Harper's Magazine Press, 1974.

Pudge Heffelfinger

Saturday Evening Post. Oct. 15, 1938, p. 14; Oct. 29, 1938, p. 16.

John Heisman

Collier's. Oct. 6, 1928, p. 12; Oct. 20, 1928, p. 14; Oct. 27, 1928, p. 12; Nov. 3, 1928, p. 18; Nov. 10, 1928, p. 12.

Herman Hickman

Coronet. Oct. 1954, p. 127.

Life. Nov. 7, 1949, p. 94.

New York Times Magazine. Oct. 28, 1951, p. 18.

Lou Holtz

Life. Sept. 1984, p. 21.

New York Times Magazine. Dec. 12, 1976, p. 63.

Reader's Digest. Sept. 1988, p. 31.

Saturday Evening Post. Sept. 1989, p. 52.

Sport. Nov. 1979, p. 19; Oct. 1987, p. 26.

Sporting News. Nov. 28, 1988, p. 12–13.

Sports Illustrated. Sept. 11, 1978, p. 40; Dec. 9, 1985, p. 24; Apr. 21, 1986, p. 34; Nov. 9, 1987, p. 26; Sept. 4, 1989, p. 38.

Time. Dec. 9, 1985, p. 77; Nov. 21, 1988, p. 148; Nov. 27, 1989, p. 90.

Jimmy Johnson

Sport. Sept. 1988, p. 60.

Sports Illustrated. Mar. 6, 1989, p. 22; Mar. 20, 1989, p. 26; Mar. 27, 1989, p. 102.

U.S. News & World Report. Sept. 11, 1989, p. 65.

Howard Jones

Bright, Chuck. *University of Iowa Football: The Hawkeyes.* Huntsville, AL: Strode Publishers, 1982.

Cohane, Tim. *Great College Football Coaches of the Twenties and Thirties.* New Rochelle, NY: Arlington House, 1973.

Coronet. Oct. 1954, p. 154.

Saturday Evening Post. Oct. 14, 1933, p. 16.

Tad Jones

Cohane, Tim. *Great College Football Coaches of the Twenties and Thirties.* New Rochelle, NY: Arlington House, 1973.

Andy Kerr

Cohane, Tim. *Great College Football Coaches of the Twenties and Thirties.* New Rochelle, NY: Arlington House, 1973.

Chuck Knox

Esquire. Oct. 1974, p. 203.

Knox, Chuck and Bill Plaschke. *Hard Knox: The Life of an NFL Coach.* San Diego, CA: Harcourt Brace Jovanovich, 1988.

Saturday Evening Post. Nov. 1974, p. 42.

Sport. Jan. 1982, p. 34.

Frank Kush

Newsweek. Oct. 26, 1970, p. 56; Oct. 29, 1979, p. 91; Nov. 23, 1981, p. 22.

Sport. Sept. 1982, p. 72; Nov. 1983, p. 94; Mar. 1985, p. 21.

Sports Illustrated. Oct. 22, 1973, p. 71; Oct. 29, 1979, p. 26; May 4, 1981, p. 9; Mar. 11, 1985, p. 34.

Tom Landry

Esquire. Oct. 1984, p. 124.

Landry, Tom with Gregg Lewis. *Tom Landry: An Autobiography.* New York, NY: Harper Collins, 1990.

Outdoor Life. Sept. 1978, p. 118.

People. Mar. 13, 1989, p. 44.

Reader's Digest. Nov. 1978, p. 227.

St. John, Bob. *The Man Inside . . . Landry.* Waco, TX: Word Books, 1979.

Saturday Evening Post. Dec. 17, 1966, p. 76; Oct. 1980, p. 62.

Sport. Sept. 1983, p. 88; Dec. 1984, p. 46.

Sports Illustrated. Sept. 18, 1972, p. 116; Dec. 21, 1987, p. 40; Nov. 14, 1988, p. 32; May 1, 1989, p. 14.

Elmer Layden

Saturday Evening Post. Nov. 6, 1937, p. 16; Nov. 26, 1938, p. 18.

Marv Levy

The Jewish Monthly. Mar. 1990, p. 22.

Frank Leahy

Collier's. Oct. 18, 1952, p. 26.

Life. Dec. 5, 1955, p. 142.

Look. Mar. 23, 1954, p. 34.

Sport. Nov. 1948, p. 16.

Twombly, Wells. *Shake Down the Thunder: The Official Biography of Notre Dame's Frank Leahy.* Radnor, PA: Chilton Publishing, 1974.

Lou Little

Cohane, Tim. *Great College Football Coaches of the Twenties and Thirties.* New Rochelle, NY: Arlington House, 1973.

Collier's. Oct. 20, 1934, p. 7; Oct. 27, 1934, p. 16; Nov. 3, 1934, p. 12.

New York Times Magazine. Nov. 18, 1945, p. 18.

Saturday Evening Post. Nov. 9, 1940, p. 35; Nov. 16, 1946, p. 16.

Vince Lombardi

Dowling, Tom. *Coach: A Season with Lombardi.* New York, NY: Norton, 1970.

Esquire. Jan. 1968, p. 68.

Flynn, George, editor. *Vince Lombardi on Football.* Greenwich, CT: New York Graphic Society, 1973.

_____. *The Vince Lombardi Scrapbook.* New York, NY: Grosset & Dunlap, 1976.

Fortune. Nov. 1968, p. 140.

Life. Sept. 27, 1968, p. 121.

Look. Oct. 24, 1961, p. 107; Sept. 19, 1967, p. 70.

Newsweek. Jan. 29, 1968, p. 75.

O'Brien, Michael. *Vince: A Personal Biography of Vince Lombardi.* New York, NY: Morrow, 1987.

Sport. Dec. 1986, p. 25.

Sports Illustrated. Sept. 9, 1963, p. 94; Jan. 2, 1967, p. 5; Mar. 3, 1969, p. 28; Jul. 28, 1969, p. 18; Jan. 27, 1986, p. 56.

U.S. News & World Report. Feb. 20, 1967, p. 14.

Dan McGugin

Cohane, Tim. *Great College Football Coaches of the Twenties and Thirties.* New Rochelle, NY: Arlington House, 1973.

John McKay

McKay, John with Jim Perry. *McKay: A Coach's Story.* New York, NY: Atheneum Press, 1974.

Newsweek. Jan. 1, 1973, p. 51; Oct. 8, 1979, p. 59.

Saturday Evening Post. Dec. 14, 1963, p. 72.

Sports Illustrated. Aug. 23, 1976, p. 16; Nov. 20, 1978, p. 88.

Time. Nov. 13, 1972, p. 77.

Tuss McLaughry

Collier's. Oct. 7, 1939, p. 21.

Bo McMillin

Collier's. Aug. 31, 1946, p. 42.

Life. Dec. 10, 1945, p. 49.

Saturday Evening Post. Sept. 28, 1946, p. 14.

John Madden

Madden, John with Dave Anderson. *One Knee Equals Two Feet (and Everything Else You Need to Know About Football).* New York, NY: Villard Books, 1986.

People. Jan. 25, 1982, p. 99.

Saturday Evening Post. Jan./Feb. 1988, p. 48.

Sport. Aug. 1983, p. 59; Jun. 1987, p. 34.

Sports Illustrated. Sept. 1, 1983, p. 38; Oct. 26, 1987, p. 106.

Time. Jan. 11, 1988, p. 82.

Johnny Majors

Majors, Johnny with Ben Byrd. *You Can Go Home Again.* Nashville, TN: Rutledge Hill Press, 1986.

Sports Illustrated. Mar. 28, 1977, p. 68; Oct. 29, 1979, p. 55.

Time. Dec. 2, 1974, p. 84.

Ted Marchibroad
   Sports Illustrated. Sept. 20, 1976, p. 49.
John Meehan
   Christian Century. Dec. 23, 1931, p. 1613.
Ron Meyer
   Sport. Jul. 1983, p. 47; Aug. 1988, p. 56.
   Sports Illustrated. Nov. 5, 1984, p. 60.
Ray Morrison
   Cohane, Tim. *Great College Football Coaches of the Twenties and Thirties.* New Rochelle, NY: Arlington House, 1973.
   Pouncy, Temple. *Southern Methodist Football: Mustang Mania.* Huntsville, AL: Strode Publishers, 1981.
Greasy Neale
   Collier's. Nov. 10, 1951, p. 30; Nov. 17, 1951, p. 24.
   Time. Nov. 12, 1973, p. 118.
Jess Neely
   Saturday Evening Post. Oct. 23, 1954, p. 26.
Robert Neyland
   Gilbert, Bob. *Neyland: The Gridiron General.* Atlanta, GA: Peachtree Publishing, 1990.
   Saturday Evening Post. Dec. 30, 1939, p. 14.
Chuck Noll
   Sports Illustrated. Jul. 21, 1980, p. 58.
   Time. Feb. 4, 1980, p. 58.
Frank O'Neill
   Outing Magazine. Oct. 1920, p. 98.
Bennie Oosterban
   Saturday Evening Post. Oct. 8, 1949, p. 38.
Tom Osborne
   Keteyian, Armen. *Big Red Confidential: Inside Nebraska Football.* Chicago, IL: Contemporary Books, 1989.
   Osborne, Tom with John Roberts. *More Than Winning.* Nashville, TN: Thomas Nelson Publishers, 1985.
   Sport. Oct. 1985, p. 50.
Steve Owen
   Collier's. Oct. 31, 1942, p. 22.
Bill Parcells
   New York. Sept. 21, 1987, p. 136.
   New York Times Magazine. Sept. 6, 1987, p. 28.
   Parcells, Bill with Mike Lupica. *Parcells: Autobiography of the Biggest Giant of Them All.* Chicago, IL: Bonus Books, 1987.
Ray Parker
   Saturday Evening Post. Nov. 13, 1954, p. 25.
   Sport. Oct. 1954, p. 80.
Ara Parseghian
   New York Times Magazine. Nov. 13, 1966, p. 56.

Pagna, Tom with Bob Best. *Notre Dame's Era of Ara.* Huntsville, AL: Strode Publishers, 1976.

Parseghian, Ara and Tom Pagna. *Parseghian and Notre Dame Football.* Notre Dame, IN: Men-In-Motion, 1971.

Saturday Evening Post. Nov. 28, 1964, p. 72; Oct. 7, 1967, p. 85.

Time. Nov. 20, 1964, p. 84; Dec. 30, 1974, p. 51.

Joe Paterno

Paterno, Joe with Bernard Asbell. *Paterno: By the Book.* New York, NY: Random House, 1989.

Reader's Digest. Nov. 1979, p. 152.

Saturday Evening Post. Oct. 1983, p. 61.

Sports Illustrated. Nov. 11, 1968, p. 19; Oct. 9, 1970, p. 44; Oct. 25, 1971, p. 24; Nov. 19, 1973, p. 46; Mar. 15, 1976, p. 40; Sept. 25, 1978, p. 34; Mar. 17, 1980, p. 34; Dec. 22–29, 1986, p. 64.

Ray Perkins

Saturday Evening Post. Dec. 1983, p. 62.

Sports Illustrated. Oct. 15, 1979, p. 34; Sept. 19, 1983, p. 80; Oct. 15, 1984, p. 80.

Bum Phillips

Esquire. Jan. 1985, p. 37.

Sport. Oct. 1980, p. 28; Sept. 1981, p. 16; Jul. 1983, p. 54.

Sports Illustrated. Nov. 3, 1975, p. 62; Oct. 27, 1980, p. 68; Jan. 29, 1990, p. 62.

Tommy Protho

Sports Illustrated. Sept. 4, 1967, p. 40; Aug. 16, 1971, p. 24.

Time. Oct. 7, 1966, p. 78; Oct. 4, 1971, p. 60.

John Ralston

Sports Illustrated. Sept. 4, 1972, p. 48.

John Rauch

Newsweek. Aug. 2, 1971, p. 83.

Dan Reeves

Reeves, Dan with Dick Connor. *Reeves: An Autobiography.* Chicago, IL: Bonus Books, 1988.

Sports Illustrated. Nov. 6, 1967, p. 28.

Eddie Robinson

Ebony. Jan. 1983, p. 60; Dec. 1985, p. 122.

Jet. Aug. 20, 1984, p. 47; Sept. 2, 1985, p. 50.

Reader's Digest. Sept. 1986, p. 113.

Sports Illustrated. Oct. 4, 1982, p. 69; Sept. 1, 1983, p. 124; Oct. 14, 1985, p. 32.

Time. Oct. 11, 1982, p. 80.

John Robinson

Sport. Feb. 1986, p. 21.

Sports Illustrated. Nov. 22, 1976, p. 46.

Knute Rockne

Brondfield, Jerry. *Rockne, The Coach, The Man, The Legend.* New York, NY: Random House, 1976.

Collier's. Oct. 18, 1930, p. 7; Oct. 25, 1930, p. 20; Nov. 1, 1930, p. 14; Nov. 8, 1930, p. 20; Nov. 15 ,1930, p. 22; Nov. 22, 1930, p. 14; Nov. 29, 1930, p. 26; Dec. 6, 1930, p. 20.

McCallum, John and Paul Castner. *We Remember Rockne.* Huntington, IN: Our Sunday Visitor, 1975.

Sports Illustrated. Sept. 10, 1979, p. 98.

Pepper Rodgers

Rodgers, Pepper and Al Thomy. *Pepper: The Autobiography of an Unconventional Coach.* Garden City, NY: Doubleday, 1976.

Darrell Royal

Sports Illustrated. Oct. 18, 1971, p. 24; Oct. 7, 1974, p. 79.

Time. Nov. 22, 1963, p. 50; Nov. 14, 1969, p. 62.

Sam Rutiglioano

Sport. Nov. 1981, p. 69; Jul. 1989, p. 12.

Buddy Ryan

Esquire. Aug. 1989, p. 49.

Newsweek. Sept. 8, 1986, p. 53.

Sport. May 1986, p. 59.

Sports Illustrated. Sept. 3, 1986, p. 116.

Lou Saban

Newsweek. Dec. 26, 1966.

People. Dec. 8, 1986, p. 167.

Sports Illustrated. Oct. 1, 1979, p. 43; Apr. 11, 1983, p. 36.

Red Sanders

Look. Nov. 17, 1953, p. 104.

Newsweek. Nov. 15, 1954, p. 100.

Saturday Evening Post. Nov. 11, 1950, p. 34.

Bo Schembechler

Schembechler, Bo and Mitch Albom. *Bo.* New York, NY: Warner Books, 1989.

Sports Illustrated. Nov. 16, 1970, p. 32; Sept. 14, 1981, p. 66; Jan. 8, 1990, p.19.

Joe Schmidt

Look. Sept. 24, 1963, p. 62.

Howard Schnellenberger

Newsweek. Jan. 16, 1984, p. 57.

Sports Illustrated. Dec. 26, 1983, p. 46.

Floyd Schwartzwalder

Saturday Evening Post. Oct. 29, 1960, p. 30.

Time. Oct. 31, 1960, p. 76.

Clark Shaughnessy

Saturday Evening Post. Nov. 1, 1941, p. 18.

Smithsonian. Feb. 1986, p. 125.

Sports Illustrated. Sept. 5, 1977, p. 90.

Jackie Sherrill

Sports Illustrated. Feb. 1, 1982, p. 26; Dec. 12, 1988, p. 78; Dec. 26, 1988, p. 24.

Don Shula
New York Times Magazine. Sept. 1, 1985, p. 14.
Shula, Don with Lou Sahadi. *The Winning Edge.* New York, NY: Dutton, 1973.
Sport. Dec. 1978, p. 26; Jan. 1983, p. 48; Nov. 1984, p. 17; Aug. 1985, p. 56; Oct. 1986, p. 53.
Sports Illustrated. Jan. 11, 1965, p. 24; Jan. 18, 1965, p. 42; Sept. 17, 1973, p. 120; Jul. 27, 1981, p. 26; Oct. 12, 1981, p. 36.
Time. Dec. 11, 1972, p. 91; Nov. 19, 1984, p. 109.

Amos A. Stagg
Reader's Digest. Feb. 1944, p. 55.
Saturday Evening Post. Sept. 18, 1926, p. 6; Oct. 2, 1926, p. 20; Oct. 9, 1926, p. 28; Oct. 16, 1926, p. 30; Oct. 23, 1926, p. 24; Oct. 30, 1926, p. 25; Nov. 6, 1926, p. 29; Nov. 13, 1926, p. 30.
Sports Illustrated. Aug. 13, 1962, p. 42.
Time. Oct. 25, 1943, p. 55.

Hank Stram
Stram, Hank with Lou Sahadi. *They're Playing My Game.* New York, NY: Morrow, 1986.

Jock Sutherland
Cohane, Tim. *Great College Football Coaches of the Twenties and Thirties.* New Rochelle, NY: Arlington House, 1973.
Saturday Evening Post. Dec. 7, 1935, p. 14.

Barry Switzer
Esquire. Dec. 5, 1978, p. 90.
Newsweek. Feb. 27, 1989, p. 80.
Sports Illustrated. Aug. 9, 1976, p. 54; Oct. 16, 1978, p. 32; Jun. 20, 1983, p. 32; Oct. 24, 1983, p. 50; Feb. 27, 1989, p. 20.

Norman Van Brocklin
Saturday Evening Post. Oct. 27, 1962, p. 74.

Johnny Vaught
Saturday Evening Post. Oct. 13, 1956, p. 33.

Wallace Wade
Cohane, Tim. *Great College Football Coaches of the Twenties and Thirties.* New Rochelle, NY: Arlington House, 1973.
Time. Oct. 25, 1937, p. 32.

Lynn O. Waldorf
Look. Oct. 23, 1951.
Saturday Evening Post. Oct. 18, 1947, p. 24.

Bill Walsh
Saturday Evening Post. Oct. 1985, p. 44.
Sport. Jul. 1983, p. 15.
Sports Illustrated. Dec. 21, 1981, p. 18; Jul. 26, 1982, p. 60; Apr. 23, 1990, p. 60.

Joe Walton
Sport. Aug. 1989, p. 50.

Pop Warner

Cohane, Tim. *Great College Football Coaches of the Twenties and Thirties.* New Rochelle, NY: Arlington House, 1973.

Collier's. Oct. 28, 1939.

George Welsh

Sports Illustrated. Sept. 20, 1982, p. 63.

Carol White

Garfield (Mass.) Reporter. Jul. 22, 1988.

People. Nov. 3, 1986, p. 63.

Sport Magazine. Sept. 1988.

Bud Wilkinson

Look. Nov. 13, 1956, p. 86; Oct. 1, 1957, p. 62.

New York Times Magazine. Nov. 9, 1958, p. 26.

Saturday Evening Post. Oct. 11, 1958, p. 31.

Sport. Aug. 1978, p. 60.

Sports Illustrated. Jul. 31, 1978, p. 20.

Sam Wyche

Sports Illustrated. Oct. 17, 1988, p. 42; Sept. 11, 1989, p. 92.

Fielding Yost

Cohane, Tim. *Great College Football Coaches of the Twenties and Thirties.* New Rochelle, NY: Arlington House, 1973.

Perry, Will. *Wolverines: A Story of Michigan Football.* Huntsville, AL: Strode, 1974.

Time. Feb. 21, 1938, p. 50.

Robert Zuppke

American Mercury. Nov. 1930, p. 18.

Index

207